copyright © jackie esse 2020

book layout and cover design by krista esse | artbykristanicole.com
interior illustrations by krista esse
back cover illustration by gigi mondragon

typeset in Fira Sans

ISBN 978-0-578-79538-6

perfectdoesntexistco.com

@ jaclynnoelle7 | @perfectdoesntexistco

~~PERFECT~~

~~DOESN'T~~

~~EXIST~~

@ jaclynnoelle7
@perfectdoesntexistco

*for the person who feels ocean-deep emotions
and isn't quite sure what to do with that*

contents

12 index

15 dear reader
16 complacency
17 "love"
19 bad again
20 I learned this from you
21 funny (?)
22 love is a terrible gamble
23 warning!!
24 nope.
26 voices in my mind
27 what if the world didn't suck
29 coffee
30 I'm smarter than you think
31 you only want me when you're drunk
32 in another lifetime
33 your scent
35 what if?
36 this is for the type A personalities
37 early august - what the fuck?
38 I bloom in the quiet
40 I'm looking for the ocean in a man
41 men are dogs
43 I didn't realize how tired I was
44 the truth is a mantra
46 3:00 am
47 coping
48 boys
50 stuck in love
51 long distance
53 7 seconds
54 the sadness stays with me when you are gone
55 glass girl
56 dam(n)
58 air is heavy
59 unspoken conversations

61 I miss the old you
62 how dare you teach me that I am an object
     designed for your pleasure
64 december 25th, 2016
66 it feels like I'm strapped to an electric chair
67 give expression
69 drunk texts
70 perfectionism
72 there's no rulebook for this
74 you are you
75 this is becoming redundant
76 I am the sun rays
78 you're wrong
79 my intuition is telling me this is coming to an end
81 your heart is worth pursuing
83 please write it down
84 you left a void
85 did medusa look at you?
86 love shouldn't be this uncertain
88 shooting stars and sea cliffs
90 I thought only my medicine gave me vertigo
92 alyssa
94 the mona lisa
96 everything pure and hoped-for
98 watch yourself
100 nothing good happens after 2 am
102 cloud of infatuation
103 I don't want you to know me anymore
104 please come back
106 the reason people stay friends
107 the lump in my throat
109 I still love you (sometimes)
111 sometimes you just need help
112 love on my mind
113 stubbornness turned out to be a good thing—
     who would've thought?
114 avoidance is my strong suit

116 blocking you was about setting boundaries
117 hit me
118 what do you want?
120 I condemn myself for being human
122 you should tell them
123 you're not that special
124 wrightwood in september
126 do you know what depression feels like?
128 unread poems
129 I would rather walk away than stoop to your level
131 our friend's death shouldn't have been used
       as a manipulation tactic
132 antisocial personality disorder
134 and that is okay
136 a series of unfortunate events: the glass girl
139 your excuses were so damn good
140 you broke my expectations and then you broke me
142 ego isn't everything
143 coming to
144 deep belly laughs
146 moving back from australia wasn't very much fun
149 silence is better than bullshit
150 bible reading shouldn't be on your chore chart
151 it wasn't worth it
152 liquid courage
154 love doesn't exist without grace
155 it is not enough to want me
157 I will not
158 learning a lesson the hard way (is hard)
159 being misunderstood hurts like a bitch
160 intimacy doesn't go away all at once
162 your coping mechanisms suck
163 I deserve an award for this
164 anesthesia
167 like a dying star
168 after death there is new life
171 go

I wrote this for you ♡
-jackie

for when your brain is mean to you
19 bad again
29 coffee
35 what if
43 I didn't realize how tired I was
46 3:00 am
53 7 seconds
58 air is heavy
66 it feels like I'm strapped to an electric chair
76 I am the sun rays
126 do you know what depression feels like?
188 panic attacks are inconvenient
207 get up

for moving on
24 nope.
31 you only want me when you're drunk
37 early august - what the fuck?
40 I'm looking for the ocean in a man
50 stuck in love
61 I miss the old you
86 love shouldn't be this uncertain
100 nothing good happens after 2 am
116 blocking you was about setting boundaries
123 you're not that special
132 antisocial personality disorder
155 it is not enough to want me

for the perfectionist
36 this is for the type A personalities
44 the truth is a mantra
70 perfectionism
198 come alive again

172 lovers OR friends
173 stay by post malone
174 kissing me was selfish
176 if I could give you all my love, I would
177 he better be pretty damn good
178 stoner mentality
180 replace me
181 ignorance is bliss
182 grace
184 emotionally unavailable
185 before the clouds came
186 exempt
188 panic attacks are inconvenient
190 the way you lost me
191 if this is love I don't want it
192 rejection doesn't phase me anymore
194 scoundrels
193 dare to be fully known
196 ew
198 come alive again
199 not now not ever
200 looks can be deceiving
201 the one thing
202 endless love
204 how dare you
205 no one can do what you can do
206 I'm starting to think nicholas sparks is a liar
207 get up
208 irreconcilable contradictions
209 (not) worth the wait
210 please let me get what I want this time
211 you're the way you are for a reason
213 perfect doesn't exist
215 you don't know me

217 acknowledgments
219 about the author

bad again

I knew it was getting bad again
three days ago
when the panic set in
I know my indicators now
and that night, I woke up every hour
to stare blankly at the ceiling
while my mind refused to stop spinning
every night since,
I haven't been able to master the art
of making my thoughts go silent in the dark
I lay hopelessly in the thickness of it
until 2 am, or 3
when it has finally simmered down a bit
because sometimes only exhaustion
makes sleep a possibility
I can finally sleep
when I have reached that miserable point;
when there is not an ounce of energy left within me
today I tried to force myself to believe
that it wasn't getting bad again
but I could see it -
like you can see a storm rolling in
I could see the clouds
I could hear the thunder
but I wanted to believe
that these indicators were merely coincidence this time
I tried to pluck my eyebrows,
a simple part of my morning routine
and the tweezers which I held within my hand
caught my eye,
for they were trembling
so *violently*
(and this made me lose my last thread of sanity)
because this time,
I thought I was okay
I wanted so badly
to just be okay

I learned this from you

there is this thing called gratitude
that makes every aspect of life
a little brighter
and a little more worth living
gratitude
has become a virtue
not a basic level of human respect as it should be
it sticks out like a ray of sunshine
when you see someone walking around
truly thankful for everything that falls into their hand
even a short conversation with a stranger
becomes something to be thankful for
I learned this from you,
and it is the most beautiful way to live life
you are walking sunlight,
filled to the brim with gratitude

funny (?)

I'd say it's funny how things change
but really
it's not funny at all
it's not funny when love starts to slip away
at first the change is gradual,
and then one day
you wake up
and what used to resemble the deepest love
has become something unrecognizable;
the person who used to think of you in everything
stopped
and although it was gradual,
now nothing is the same
it isn't funny how things change,
it is many things:
frightening
disorienting
heart-wrenching
but no,
it is not funny

love is a terrible gamble

being in love with your best friend
is the only form of love I am interested in
it is the exception;
the only gamble that will ever be worth the risk
you pulled me into an ocean of love with you,
making the jump, yet not in totality
(though it seemed to be at first)
but something changed there in the water
you were fully immersed in the depth of it
and for some reason,
that changed everything
I've experienced the worst of it
because love is a terrible gamble
and I've lost
I remain here, in the same place,
and I wonder
if love could ever be worth this loss
you've moved far from the place you ended things upon
but my heart is unmoving, my emotions are unwavering
and I'll have to be carried away
for I've remained paralyzed
ever since that day

warning!!

a lot of people are scared to love
some people just don't care to love
don't mistake love for apathy,
there are only so many chances that you should give
your heart is capable of offering forgiveness freely
you pour out grace from the depths of you,
and you are so strong for this
but has anyone told you
that you shouldn't give your kindness
to the kind of man
that will take advantage of your heart
because he'll break it, and he'll change it
don't let him rob you of the way you love
guard your gentless,
guard your heart from men like this
you might carry the capacity for grace
but that does not mean
that you should let destructive things
close enough to break you

nope.

you think that you can come in
and out
asking for more -
but I am not a door
that you can walk through
coming and going
as you please
you see,
loving passively
is not love at all
if your aim is to love conveniently
then I beg you
keep your apathy away from me
if that is the extent of your love,
I don't want it

voices in my mind

Jesus please forgive me
for falling short in loving them
I am haunted by voices
resounding inside of my mind
proclaiming over and over again
that I am not good enough, that I can never mess up,
perfection is what I must attain,
unworthy of human connection, I remain
but I know these are all lies
circling around my brain
day after day
show me grace,
one moment at a time
show me how to love them better
and by grace,
I know I'll be alright
teach me to live inside these rhythms
of messing up,
and then trying again
constantly wrapped within love
and understanding
that nothing is at stake
I am free to be human here
in this place
residing forever
within grace

what if the world didn't suck

I wish that boys
loved girls
the way that good men
love their daughters
it would be far simpler that way,
and the world
would be a much better place

coffee

coffee with cream
in the morning
the way they swirl at first
and then become one
although it can be seen as the joining of things,
I could only focus on the way
that the purity of the white was swallowed up
completely
and it reminded me of the way I have lost myself
in this illness
and
in you
the way a person can be dissolved
into an abyss
and what was once light
can be clothed
in darkness
the loss of myself
feels so absolute
like cream dissolving into coffee
in an irreversibly harsh
finality

I'm smarter than you think

I cannot possibly understand
this thing our generation is infatuated with;
meaningless pleasure
meaning and authenticity are so central to me
like blood runs through my veins
so runs authenticity
I desire something too deep
to settle for a hollowed out version of love
I do not want to kiss you
if you do not see *me*
it doesn't matter what you say -
I can feel that there is no meaning
in your body against mine
I can feel all that this is lacking
and this was never my intention,
to kiss you with no meaning
men are constantly undermining
a woman's sense of intuition
but I know the second something is wrong
I can feel your heart shifting
it's bleeding out
in your actions, in your voice
in your breath against mine
I can feel this has lost all meaning
it wouldn't make a difference
if it was me or the next girl
and I have no interest in something like that -
something that is painfully void

you only want me when you're drunk

I was desperate to kiss you that night
one more time
but you stared into my eyes
and I had to look down
I will not do this to myself
not now, not again
I am worth far more
than an undisputedly meaningless
simple
drunken kiss

in another lifetime

I'm starting to think that these poems,
are merely desperate cries to get you to stay,
masked as threats of leaving
but they are really only empty
what do I know
when I am weak and wounded?
tonight I am struck down
and my heart is still crying out for you
but tomorrow when I wake up with soreness in my spirit
from the trauma which I have endured
I will remember my worth
I will remember that I do not want toxic things
so no,
I do not want you
even though it hurts to lose you
I do not want you
I want a different version of you -
the one who does not treat me like this
I want the version of you who wipes my tears,
reads my poems
and listens to me crying at 2 am through the phone
I want the person you used to be
not the one who neglects me
wounds me
and carries too much pride
to say you're sorry that you hurt me
I do not want you,
I want the version of you who loved
and pursued me
relentlessly
it's terrifying, isn't it?
the way it all shifts
I wonder if it's possible
to be safe in the hands of another
who forever carries the potential
of changing their mind about loving you

your scent

I hate that I woke up today
with your scent still lingering on my clothes
because I am reminded
even after all that has happened
that I cannot have you
and I cannot run into your arms again
the scent of you
disturbs me so intensely
because it is one more thing
among the hundreds of others
that takes my mind back to you

what if?

I live within a constant state of dread
fearing what has not yet been,
fearing what may never happen
I am robbed of experiencing reality
because of this thing called anxiety
it is stealing my moments,
and overwhelming my peace
I am living within a paralyzing terror
because my mind is predispositioned
to rest within this state
I just want to experience the now
I want this fear to flee
but an incessant question
hangs over me:
what if?

this is for the type A personalities

for those who believe that nothing they do
will ever be good enough
for the ones who crumble beneath the standards
they themselves set
for the ones who are exhausted from the pressure
of living another day
underneath this overwhelming weight
I promise,
no one is harder on yourself than you
you are not what you do;
you are not merely what you accomplish
your worth is not a sum total
of every good thing you have produced
your worth is not measured by success
you are not a machine,
you are a human
and perfection
can never be attained
stop crumbling beneath the weight
stop bowing underneath the pressure
live instead under grace
because your worth is not weighed
by what comes out of you
do your best,
and leave it at that
you are not what you do,
you are worth so much more than that

early august - what the fuck?

we stopped making out,
and you stopped making time for me
so let me ask you this one thing:
where the hell are your priorities?

I bloom in the quiet

I fell in love with my own company
I found myself in the quiet
when I took time to let my soul breathe,
write
and scream
I found myself in the healing
that could only be found in the absence of busyness
and the loneliness
that is not so lonely anymore
I enjoy my own company now
and this empowers me to say no
to those who are not worth all that I give them
to those who trample and abuse me
I will not give my heart to those undeserving
just because I do not want to be alone
and there is immense power in that
I do not need those who only abuse and neglect,
and mistreat me
day after day
I will grow alone
I will grow apart from anyone else
I've fallen in love with the quiet
my soul needs it to breathe
to be
and to write
I bloom in the quiet
in the dark of which I am not afraid anymore
it's an amazing feeling
to have conquered the fear of being alone
my mind could be alone for days on end
and not grow weary
but I do need you
when that time runs out

and I've decided that I want to be human,
with humans
once again
there's life in that too
both in the quiet
and with you

I'm looking for the ocean in a man

that was lust, not love
and let me tell you
how utterly uninterested I am
in anything that does not have meaning
I am looking for the ocean in a man
I refuse to let you use me
as the means to satisfy a desire
I could feel it in the way you kissed me
the way you held me said that you wanted something
it wasn't enough,
just you and me kissing slowly
and I was desperate to find our intimacy again
so I kissed you, naively
even when you were like this
I thought it meant something
until I felt in your body
that your heart was unattached from what we were doing
and that might feel good to my flesh,
but my soul was aching
I could feel it in the way you touched me
I missed you, so I let it happen
but I had to learn
that I could have your body,
but your heart would remain far from everything that I need
and *you* would remain far from me
so I told you not to kiss me,
unless you were willing to be committed to me
and I realized that we were over
before the night ever began

men are dogs

when I got old enough
my dad took me on a walk
for the sole purpose of explaining to me
one simple concept
he said to me,
men are dogs
and to them,
you are a piece of meat
the concept sounded so extreme
but since that moment in time
no one has ever come close
to changing my mind

I didn't realize how tired I was

an unmade bed
rests in the center of the room,
attesting to my newfound depression
neglected laundry is sprawled atop every surface
as if an explosion happened
I have been waking up at noon,
thoroughly exhausted
I am so exhausted
I am deprived of life, it seems
but this is not me
I want to scream
and I do not want this to be my reality
I so desperately strive to do everything perfectly
yet lately,
I cannot seem to get out of bed
or accomplish *any* of my responsibilities
when will this constant sense of fatigue
stop lingering over me?
it is not normal
to wake up feeling like I've been hit by a truck
not once or twice this week,
but every morning
a weight holds me to the mattress
gravity even
has become heavy

the truth is a mantra

for the days you are down on yourself,
because you are not better, stronger
smarter or wiser
know that you are more than what you produce
and the beauty of your soul
is made of more than the looks of you
as negativity attempts to triumph over your thoughts,
know that the spirit of God lives within you
he is the truth
and the truth will set you free
for the moments you compare,
for the moments you don't measure up
may you immerse yourself in truth
and may the spirit of God begin to lift you up
out of this place of despondency,
comparison,
and wretched thinking
you are beloved,
you are seen
you are pursued in the midst of imperfection
"while we were still sinners, Christ died for us"
remember there is no perfect mark for you to meet

you are delighted in,
regardless of all that is flawed within you
regardless of how you are seen
you were chosen,
before you were made perfect and whole
know that you are seen
through the eyes of perfect love and unending grace
and the only weight bringing you down
lives within your mind
but the spirit of God lives within you too,
so simply ask for him to change you
ask for his voice to be louder than the enemy's,
louder than your own,
louder than people who surround you
give him the megaphone that resounds over your life
for this is how it was always meant to be;
his voice carries the truth,
and the truth will set you free
just let him speak

3:00 am

I've come to resent 3 am
because it is familiar
because there are not far more than 2 consecutive hours
in which I might remain sleeping without interruption
I wish I could wake up feeling rested
but enduring nights like these
is no easier than rigorous activity
I am anything but rested when I wake
the only good I feel
is a slight sense of relief
that I have made it through another night
the light streaming through my window tells me
that I can now resort to doing anything other
than tossing and turning underneath my sheets
this relief is fleeting,
because even getting out of bed
requires insurmountable effort
when rest has left the equation,
when all that is left is exhaustion -
I want to feel like a person again
I want to experience daylight
without a heaviness in my spirit,
without bags under my eyes

coping

I fell into a pit
in which
empty things
became my coping mechanism
but I am a person created for depth
I chase meaning,
I chase feeling and feeling deeply
I have been sitting in a dark room
with empty things surrounding me
and I've decided that I do not want the emptiness anymore
I want the meaning and the feeling
even if it means hurting,
even if it means breaking open
after all of this time,
after all of this suppressing
I am returning to myself,
I am climbing out

boys

to put off a persona of safety
is what boys love to do
they carry ocean-deep promises in empty words
making a fool of devotion, love,
and commitment
they carry the facade of a grown man,
who is capable of these things
and they like what their promises do to you
so
striking a match
they hold promises like fire up to your hardened heart
and with every whisper, more and more wax melts,
now you are soft to their touch
you bend at their will,
folding and leaning into the trap which was strung for love
they have you where they want you:
at their disposal
but dare you ask something of them
the day will come
when you hold the promises they once made
in front of their eyes
and ask for the follow through -
but this is the very moment
where the fire has reached the end of the stick
crumbling to ash
and taking your hope with it

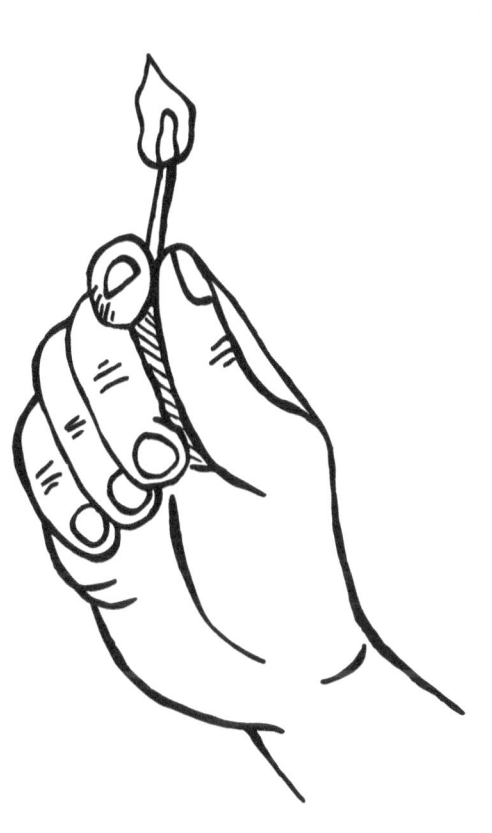

stuck in love

I love him so much that it hurts
who would have ever thought
that I would become this person?
this was never me
losing myself
consumed in him
I was never the girl
who was weak when it came to men
I try to be strong
but he melts me
he melts all that is stubborn and arrogant within me
it is so easy for him
to draw me in
I love even the unlovable pieces of me and him,
interwoven
after all this time,
after all that has happened
I find myself here
loving him so much that it hurts
and that frustrates me immeasurably

long distance

when I lose someone
whether it be a friend
or a lover
I cannot help but mourn over the reality
that I do not get to hold their heart in my hands any
longer
I do not get to do life knowing their soul anymore
and that, I think,
is the most dreadful part
I do not get to know them
not in that way
I can love from a distance
but never the same

7 seconds

I am a spectator of my own life
I couldn't sleep right last night,
another symptom that it's all happening again;
that it's getting bad again,
this sickness in my mind
I woke up every hour and stared at my ceiling
wide awake,
wondering what a life would be
without this monster living inside my head
unrelenting,
even in my sleep
I start pleading,
haven't you taken enough of my days and hours away
that were meant to be lived in solitude and peace?
if you insist on coming at all,
leave the night to me
can I just have this one thing?

when the morning finally comes,
I sit at a windowsill
watching the rain
conscious that the storm is rolling in
thunder cracks,
7 seconds between this time
panic will soon set in
and I am completely detached
from any possibility of making it stop
I am a spectator of my own body and mind
so I sit watching the clouds come slowly over the house,
listening to the rain go drip drop
I hear the thunder crack, and count to three
waiting to be overcome
by this familiar storm called anxiety

the sadness stays with me when you are gone

if I could walk away from my emotions
the way I can walk away from you
life would be far simpler
but this sadness stays with me,
even when you are gone
this wanting stays with me,
even when it's late
even when I should be sleeping
I cannot simply choose to stop feeling this
or to forget
but I can walk away from you
and one day,
the memory of this wound
will grow dim
subduing you
to nothing greater
than insignificant

glass girl

jackie you're fragile
and I know you hate this about yourself,
but you are
and it's not a bad thing
I cried after this defining statement was made
because of all of the pain fragility has caused me,
because of the truth it held
and the weight
I cried because I wish I did not have to be like this
thick skin is not for me
with sarcasm, maybe
but not when life hits,
and not emotionally
this fragile heart needs to be loved by soft words
and gentle hands
but this is not a strength common to men
I know this
because I have been loved in harshness,
loved
by men too weak to be gentle

dam(n)

the wall which once held my feelings in
collapsed
like a dam breaking open,
water which was long suppressed
violently rushed forth
passing down the hillside
collecting in puddles at the bottom;
my heart spilled out
and now,
I am spending my days trekking slowly up the hill
with one single bucket
pouring the water back into confinement, as it once was held
painfully conscious of the weight it required to be vulnerable
(before this fell apart,
before it tore me apart)
and now,
the weight it requires to be vulnerable once again
I am putting my heart back together
this requires time and effort
and I question whether I have the capacity for it
but even if this process takes months,
I will be whole once again
if you are undergoing this journey,
every step you take and every weight you carry is worth it
because you are fighting
to love wholeheartedly once again
even if that means climbing this mountain with one single bucket
one thousand times
and then again

air is heavy

moments have become exhaustingly heavy
air even,
is heavy
my limbs are full of lead
and boulders rest on my chest
ever since depression came to visit me
breathing does not feel good
when my lungs are filled
not with oxygen,
but anxiety
when a moment should contain joy
I remain here and let it pass by
because 5 minutes have burned up
while I was trying to conjure the strength to get up
while I was attempting to send my thoughts onto a productive chain
I failed,
and I am sitting here still
trying to escape the heaviness
lifting this incessant weight is exhausting
and precious seconds and minutes are fleeting
I am being robbed of meaning
because I cannot find the will to do anything
the morning is the worst,
I cannot get out of bed
because everything holds an insurmountable weight
even moments,
even this poem
is like lifting boulders to create

unspoken conversations

I held your hand in the car that night
because it was familiar,
because I needed a way to show my affection for you
I needed some part of me to believe that this wasn't over
I kept thinking maybe it was wrong
that you'd get upset with me for it
because you were the one who ended things
but the second I moved my hand towards you,
you grabbed it
so quickly
and you wouldn't let go even when I would lessen my grip,
just to test what your reaction would be
I want all of you
and right now I am hungry
for the pieces I've been getting
I know this is enough for tonight
but later down the road
it will not be enough
to have you
but only in fragments

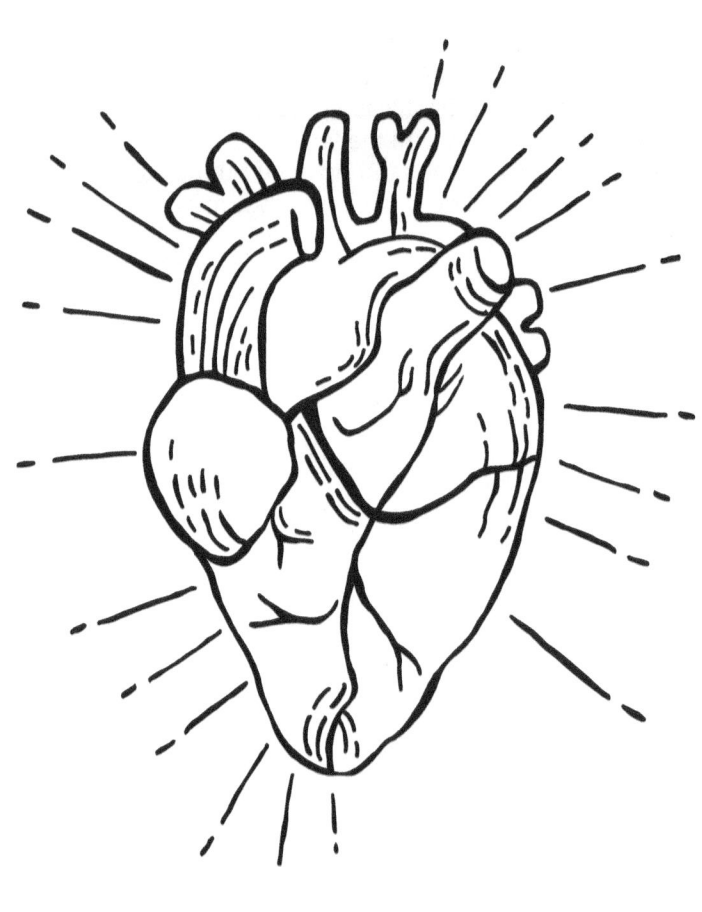

I miss the old you

your body does not mean anything to me
if your heart is unattached
I am completely uninterested
in anything that is surface level
I want love,
not lust
do not kiss me
if you are unwilling to give me that depth
do not kiss me
with the expectation of satisfying your momentary desire
and then walking away idly
it might be lost in our society,
but kissing is still intimacy to me
so if this is really you,
find someone who values what you do
and do not come back to me
do not come back
without your heart
without commitment
I will not be used to satisfy this moment
ridden of meaning, reeking of pleasure
I will not be found in your sheets

how dare you teach me that I am an object designed for your pleasure

he knows the right things to say
to get a girl to stay,
and to open her legs
but he picks up and leaves when he wants to
it's manipulative
it's wretched
and downright deceptive
it's disgusting
what sex has been resorted to
the things boys would do
to get what they want from you
makes me lose my faith in men

I'm telling you now,
you have to know your worth apart from him
you must be filled by something else
or he will come along
and draw you in
with words sweeter than honey
he will whisper the compliments
and promises
that you have been desperate to hear
and he will whisper it *exactly*
the way you want him to
only to take what he wants from you
and to leave when he is through

he is looking to be filled
and you are too
but sustenance isn't found this way
giving your bodies to each other
to satisfy a craving
or perhaps as a coping mechanism
taking the significance out of something beautiful
will not fill your soul
you'll be emptier when it is all done
and when the moment is over
he'll be gone too,
like a vapor in the wind

it is not meant to be this way
your body is meant to be given
to the one who will cherish you
know your worth,
know your worth apart from him
so that when he comes around,
whispering sweet nothings
they will truly be nothing
holding no significant weight
when whispered to your ears
and you will be able to walk away
unwavering in your profound understanding
of how much you are truly worth,
you will be able to walk away

december 25th, 2016

I remember that day,
the day we lost you
you can find me in the stars,
you said
once before you left
and when the day came
that you were no longer on this earth
I looked heavenward and cursed the sky
for it was full of clouds,
and not a single star was in sight
the malicious clouds
thickly coated the heavens
and I could not see a thing
no glimmer of hope was shining down
no comfort was found
where is he?
show me him in the stars,
I pleaded
but you were nowhere to be found
I cursed the wretched sky,
though I kept heaven in mind
and I still look for you in the stars sometimes

you're the brightest one
as you glimmer down
I can see your head-tilted smile in the brilliance of it
the goofiness, the jawline
the youthfulness of you
I didn't understand why you had to go then,
on a day meant to be filled with so much joy
I couldn't fathom why you weren't found in the sky
it was hard for me to breathe
it was hard for me to sing

I could barely eat
nothing about that dark day made sense
yet on the other side of eternity
there was glorious celebration
King Jesus brought you home to him on his birthday
receiving the best gift that could have ever been offered;
his beautiful son in glory
heaven was roaring in celebration,
on earth all we saw was mourning
I love you, Matthew
I'll see you sparkling in the sky and say goodnight
you really are the most beautiful star
thank you for protecting me,
even on the other side of eternity

it feels like I'm strapped to an electric chair

an electric current pulses through me
draining me of all energy
you may know it too,
what it's like
to fight fatigue just to survive
to wake up in the middle of the night
for the millionth time
wanting to scream
raging out against this thing
that is embedded so deeply within
this friction, this frustration that you feel
I know it is tearing you up inside
I know it is eating you alive
but you feel this pain because you are still fighting
after all this time,
you have never accepted defeat
you have stood strong against it all
you are fortified like steel
you are stronger than you feel
these flames have not consumed you
instead you have been refined,
into a great force to be reckoned with
my dearest, you fight just to survive
and that makes you strong beyond measure
not weak

give expression

when I read poetry
I feel at home in the world
I finally understand that I am not alone
in the way I feel, or in the way I love
I'm not alone in the way my heart breaks
or in the way I lie awake at night
or even in the way
that it feels impossible to move on from a lost love
I feel like I belong
now that I have found this community,
now that I have found this home
these poems are a lifeline
telling me I am not alone
in the way I see and experience the world
I only wish someone had told me sooner,
that there is a place for me among these poets
and that I can find home in the poems
I wish I knew that
when I was lying awake in my room
years ago,
aching from deep within my heart
wondering why it feels like my emotions are heightened
and how,
how it could ever be possible
to cope with feeling things this deeply
with seeing the world this way
going through life emotionally
what I have learned is this;
give your emotions expression,
or you will corrupt your solitude
and you will die with these things unfelt,
unknown,
and unkind
lingering still,
in the deep recesses of your mind

you shouldn't have to get drunk
to show me this kind of affection
if you cannot be man enough to face your fears
if you cannot tell me how you really feel
in the daylight, and straight to my face
then you need to take your affection
to a different place
I won't settle for your drunk texts
I'll wait for a man who is strong enough
to step into that fear
and I will not settle for less

    - drunk texts

perfectionism

I'm afraid of the pressure
I'm afraid of the eyes
I'm afraid of learning that every good thing I hoped I would be
is merely a figment of my imagination,
and not reality
I crumble beneath the pressure;
I do not want to fail in front of them,
but more than that,
I do not want to fail in front of myself
no one on earth will ever be so hard on me
as me
perhaps this comes with a type a personality
no accomplishment is good enough
to meet the standards which I myself have set
I am condemning,
I am anything but gracious
and I am *crumbling*
underneath the standard of perfection
that only I have set

I cannot accept even the gentlest criticism
because whatever you have pointed out
is less than adequate within me,
I can guarantee,
I have already spent countless moments
abusing myself
for not being greater than
I expect perfection
I promise that your standards
are not higher than my own
if I have hurt you deeply,
it is fair to believe
that I remind myself of it
daily
I am not perfect in loving
I am not perfect in anything
this is not enough for me
and I am crumbling,
beneath the weight of perfectionism

the perfection of Jesus
is the only thing that can save anyone from this weight
may his abounding grace
begin to surround us
in these moments of crumbling beneath this impossible standard
may we be reminded
that we live within his perfection,
his righteousness
is there anything on earth more beautiful than that?
he has taken the weight
and we can breathe easier knowing
it is not up to us to be perfect
we simply rest in his finished work,
mindful of the weighty sacrifice
that perfect love
and unending grace
won for us
that we might live abundantly

there's no rulebook for this

it is far easier
to let go of a lover
than a friend
the friendships I have lost
still come knocking on the door of my heart
as I sit and gaze,
pondering if there could ever be a way
for us to be friends again
to restore what was once lost
in the midst of toxicity and lies and selfishness
I do not hold anger,
instead I hold an unwavering hope
that continuously returns to me,
asking,
could we please try again?
with a lost lover, however,
there is a window of opportunity
a timer that has been set
a clock ticking down
for them to come around
for them to love me right
and if they do not make it
the window will close
- never to be opened again
I do not know how to reconcile these patterns of behavior
when I fell in love with my best friend
and the love came back around
unrequited
see,
I have lost him
but my heart cannot decide
whether I should treat him
as a lover
or as a friend

you are you

whether people know you,
whether they don't,
it's important to know
you are not anyone's perception of you;
you are you
whether lies have circulated around your name
whether the words spoken over you ring throughout your brain
the perception of others does not define your identity
that is,
if you do not let it shape you
you must choose to not let it change you
you must find out who you are and hold onto it tightly
resolving to be loyal to your true self
refusing to mold into anyone's perception of you
and rejecting false definitions of your identity
if you are bold
do not let the voice of the one who calls you shy
quiet your voice
and resound loudly within your mind
if you are a spitfire
a warped perspective
cannot stifle the boldness of that spirit
remember who you are
and be careful to not let anyone corrupt your identity
because you are not anyone's perception of you,
you are you

this is becoming redundant

again and again I spin
within this cycle of toxicity
returning to those who have hurt me
feeding myself into the mouths of young lions
willingly
I plead with myself,
interrupt this cycle,
would you just interrupt it
but when loneliness comes knocking
when my heart tells me insistently
that they cannot be that bad
that things could be better this time
I listen
when loneliness has worn me down
and my soul is desperate for connection
I listen

I am the sun rays

depression and anxiety
cast a somber shadow over me
and my true self,
which is bright and full of life
was afflicted with darkness
and thus I grew,
acquainted and familiar,
I grew accustomed to myself like this;
afflicted by anxiety,
not quite me
not quite who I used to be
not as bright, nor as whole
and I could hardly recognize my true identity
in the thickness of the resistance
that plagued me every day
and kept me up most nights
but I have realized one thing,
and this one thing changes everything:
I am not this person made dull
as though a light bulb covered by a sheet
I am what is underneath
unconfined,
unweighted
by anything
I am the sun rays
I am the smile
although this cloud hangs over me,
I remain the person unattached to this suffering
I am who I am
when the storm has passed away,
I am the sun rays

you're wrong

it might feel
like your chest is being ripped open,
because your once indestructible hopes have been obliterated
in unfairness, in totality
subdued to the thin crisp of burnt ashes
it may feel like no one will ever love you again,
or like your love will go unmet for an eternity
that you'll be lying on your deathbed, love unrequited
right about yourself,
right all along
but the truth is
you are wrong about yourself
how you feel
is not all that is real
your chest is not being crushed by stones
you can breathe here
and you can hope again, you can dream even
somewhere in the midst of this
you'll find flickers of light shining in
illuminating the despair with hope
you have a future beyond these despondent thoughts,
beyond this hole your spirit is resting in
after you've felt this for a little while
you will become stronger again
because He will make you strong
you will be strong enough to rise
to be filled with life
to be inspired, elated
walking around wide-eyed
full of joy
carrying an astounding inclination
to be tuned-in to beautiful things
all of this will be restored within you once again
you may have lost someone,
or something
but all hope is not lost
this despair is only a season
and the light will stream in all the more boldly this time

my intuition is telling me this is coming to an end

would you whisper the phrase
I'm yours
if you did,
I think every fiber in my being
would both explode
and melt
into incandescence
because then we could start living the adventure of love
that I keep worrying we will never have

boys get distant
when relationships get deep
while men pursue depth
   intentionally
your heart is worth pursuing
always remember that
   whoever loves you
   and whoever doesn't
will never determine your worth

please write it down

I would give you a notebook
and ask you to fill it
with what you could never admit
in the light of day
with everything you could never quite say
straight to my face;
or untangle within the chaos that resides
within your heart and mind
I would give you this notebook
bound in brown leather
and I would ask you to fill it
with words more valuable than treasure
asking that in this time away,
you would write in it everything you cannot say
in this season of breaking me mercilessly
I would ask you to fill it
yet sadly,
I suspect it would remain empty
and I would remain despondent
for you would only return blank lines
or ones filled with lies
when all I have ever asked for is honesty
I write this poem,
because the idea of a little leather notebook
containing letters from you to me
filled with truth and meaning
is a concept that will live in my mind;
something that will never come to life

you left a void

what do you do
when the person you used to run to
cannot hold themselves up
and they unquestionably cannot hold you
tell me,
who do I run to
when I'm aching for your arms
I am aching for your affirmation
and the gentleness with which you loved me
the magnitude and the depth
that are so absent now
all that is left is a void
in the place that love and care
used to so bountifully reside

did medusa look at you?

surely you have wronged me,
if you have treated me in apathy
for nothing stings worse
than giving your all
to a person incapable of love and feeling
someone refusing to move
no matter what you do
I may as well have poured my time
and whispered the deepest longings of my heart
to a statue
because the reactions would have stayed just the same
I could hit you and you would not move to stop me
I could leave and you would not reach out your arm to grab me
I could cry my eyes out before you,
telling you of all the ways
your lifelessness
is ripping my heart out,
yet still you would remain
stone cold and lifeless
unmoving,
as a statue
I may as well have loved a man made of stone,
for at least then
he would not have promised me empty things

love shouldn't be this uncertain

did he love me,
did he not?
were genuine emotions
ever truly there?
for I felt the sea between him and me
the great ocean waves sent a buzzing,
a loving
and with each ripple that came and crashed into my chest,
I was hit with a blissful happiness
(lighter than sea spray)
produced by the crash of the waves
only the force of the great ocean
could contain what I felt for him
in ripples and in waves
the magnitude of it came,
yet never did it simply pass through -
it wasn't a coming and a going
never
could it be resorted to a fleeting feeling
because I was completely immersed
in love for him
in love with him
and the waves only exemplified that
with a humming, a buzzing
and a sea of raging emotions breaking within me like
waves
just like the next ripple,
you rushed towards me
whispering sweet nothings
which were softer than seafoam

and gentler than anything I had ever known
I felt the sea
between you and me
but did you ever feel anything?
and if you did,
was it simply a fleeting feeling
lost in the memory
of you and me,
hanging on a surfboard in the middle of the sea
dreaming of a serendipity
that would never be reality
just you and me and the waves
you whispered,
but as quickly as the water reached my feet
you returned back to the sea:
an ocean wave that came
and then was lost again

shooting stars and sea cliffs

you immortalized that year;
the year I was 17
those memories will always be looked back on
blanketed in golden rays of sunshine
full of starlight
and the innocence of young minds
young hearts living reckless and wild
I'll remember you in the shooting stars
the sunsets and sea cliffs
and the one you engraved,
just a boy
just 17
I'll find you especially
in the still summer nights of July
where possibilities were endless
freedom was at our fingertips
you were an incredible friend to me
my protector
you will always be,
even though now it is from the sky
I pray to God and ask him to say hi
and to tell you all of the things I never got to say
but I'll see you again one day,
and apologies won't be on my mind

just you and I reunited
and you'll introduce me to all of the saints you've met,
all of your friends in heaven
because you were always good
at making friends
you were always exceptional
at making everyone feel welcome
it's lucky, that you got to eternity first
you didn't have to experience what it feels like
when your family in Christ leaves your side
I'm glad for it,
that at least you didn't ever have to feel this loss
you're up there covered in immeasurable joy
no one deserves it more than your pure heart
better than an angel, you're a saint
glorified,
whole in the presence of Christ

I thought only my medicine gave me vertigo

we fell apart
faster than I could blink
or think twice
you wrapped me in a whirlwind
of uncertainty and chaos
now I'm waiting for everything to stop spinning
and for everything to stop hurting
my heart has taken so many beatings
that it is barely functioning
and I cannot see

outside of this dizziness

that you have left me in

alyssa

it was her, it was her
it was always, always her
except for when it wasn't, except for when it was me
except for when you were pleading
confessing that it was me,
that it had always been me
please believe me this time,
you said
again and again
promising so insistently
that I began to believe
it was me, it was me
it was always, always me
and it was never ever her
because those were *your* words
after your pleading, after your convincing
when I finally felt safe
serendipity was interrupted
by that godforsaken name
oh that godforsaken name
which interrupted our confessions
and came into the midst of bliss
a hitch in our flow
caused by the thought of her
and those weighty conversations began

because maybe it was her, it was her
and never, ever me
it was never me
why would I believe it would be?
I was trapped, I was schemed
because you -
you manipulated my thoughts
and my feelings
to get the outcome you wanted
as each moment came
because to you
love is a game
and the truth was revealed
by something as simple
as a name
no,
the fault could never be hers
it was yours

if he were to walk
    away from you

my dear

it would be as if he left

the Mona Lisa

in the rain

and you —

are the most
    exquisite painting

everything pure and hoped-for

you are the kind of woman
whose heart radiates the essence of femininity and beauty
sensationally
this heart requires a man to love it, for a boy could never hope to
he wouldn't know the first thing about loving you
and he knows it, he is profusely,
utterly
aware of this
you might have thought,
somewhere along the way
rejection after rejection
that you were not good enough
but the truth is
that you are the type of woman
whose very presence asks for more respect and dignity
than a boy could ever hope to give you
it is not your imperfection that caused him to turn away
you were everything,
you were ready
and because of the transparency of your soul,
and the dignity which you so gracefully bring into every room
he turned away
not because you were not enough,
extravagantly, you embodied everything pure and hoped-for
and he was less than willing to accept the challenge of growing up
to give a woman what she really deserves,
he knew deep down that he couldn't keep you
radically petrified by this
his fear of failure was all consuming,
like a flame it licked up all that was once brave within him
he would rather walk away
than try to win your heart
only to be overwhelmed by his shortcomings
see

it wasn't you after all
he's afraid that *he* is not enough
you are undisputedly worthy
altogether, unconditionally
enough

watch yourself

we must be increasingly careful
to not look at a person's exterior
and then go on assuming
that we know what their heart looks like
we must be slow to get angry
because maybe,
just maybe
they are not treating you like they used to

because they are drowning in their circumstances
maybe it is not you
and you should, instead of growing angry,
become increasingly more patient
being mindful that their pain
is bigger than the way it affects you
we must be careful not to assume
that we know a person is happy
because they carry the beautiful delight
of a laughter that rings within, and resounds throughout,
every room they walk into
those who are seemingly happy
are often unbearably depressed
maybe that person who is hard on the outside
only carries that exterior
because they have been abused, consistently,
and they do not know how else to protect
their fragile heart
they are not hard,
they are soft
and their softness was taken advantage of
and tainted
we must be slow to judge
we must stop judging altogether,
because it is not our place
and we do not know the hearts of those
who walk around this world in close proximity to us
though their exterior is seen
you cannot possibly know their interior
be quick to show grace
quick to love
be increasingly quicker, not to judge,
but to silence the voice that tells you
that you know what their heart looks like
when only God does
and he loves them abundantly, endlessly
you see,
people are not our enemy

nothing good happens after 2 am

nothing has ever felt more right
than your hand in mine
but you are taking me on this roller coaster,
back and forth you are swinging me
because you don't know what to do
yet all I want
is to be with you
none of this is fair to me
please silence this misery
I am not strong enough to do it
if I am left to myself
every night
I will run back to you

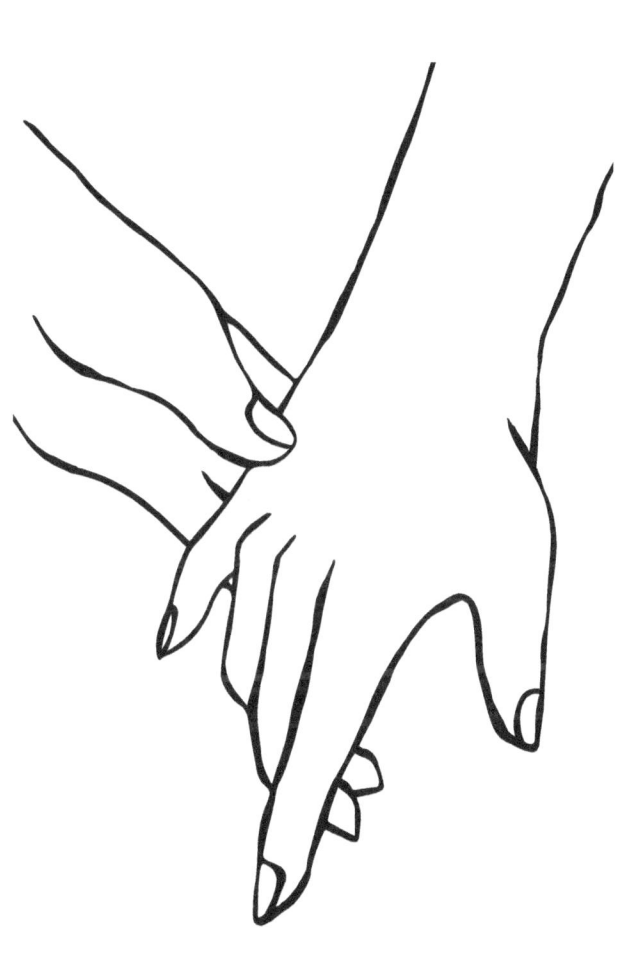

cloud of infatuation

it's terrifying how reality becomes blurred
when infatuation sets in
I thought the reason I had so many poems about you
was because you were significant
but I am realizing
the only thing that is significant about our love
is the magnitude of pain you have caused me;
the love poems were written in naivety
and the rest
were simple expressions of pain
and longing
no, it is not you who was significant
but rather, the way you broke me

I don't want you to know me anymore

I whispered
I think I'm in love with you
you said you could tell
because I wrote poems about you
and that made me feel like hell
I thought that was incredibly arrogant to admit
it made me feel sick
because just last week
you said the same about me,
even when I was not ready
and you said
you wanted to marry me
yet now,
you are running from authenticity
it was in this moment of transparency
that I noticed your heart was shifting away from me
and I know now
that mine is not safe with you
anymore
I do not want you to see into my heart
as through a clear piece of glass
be careful with your words
because if you keep saying things like that
I'll start to make the glass hazy
until all there is
is black
my *I'm in love with you's*
are not something that you should take for granted
they're like shooting stars
rare, and sought after
and they should never
be ignored

please come back

my heart is drifting away from you
you,
who once became home to me
you were once my safe place
embodying kindness, love, strength,
compassion, and dignity
so beautifully
those things are still there
and trust me, I do not hate you
I love you more than I love most people on this earth
but you're breaking me
my heart and my trust
there are more cracks every day
and all you have to do is spread the glue and let it dry
but you're pulling my pieces apart over and over again
before they've ever had the chance to
my confidence in you is fleeting
there was a time where I had a raging passion
for what was between us
this kept me from being passive
refusing to watch us crumble in apathy,
I burned brightly for you, for us,
carrying a fervency for our love
but you're smothering us,
throwing a blanket over it
you're not tending to it anymore, you're killing it
and I am crying in my room at 11:52
because I don't want to find a home in anyone else
not now, not ever
but my fire is being put out
by you
I cannot keep the embers hot
when you are pouring out water,
when you are working against me

I wish you cared half as much as me
your words don't make me blink anymore
you said yourself,
the day will come when you regret letting me go
you'll regret your lack of love too
maybe by then I will not have moved on
but I owe it to myself to not linger here any longer
I cannot see you as my home
I will miss you terribly
please come back to me
(before it's too late)

the reason people stay friends

romance and risk coexist
but with you, I am stuck on safety
I have pictured being married to you countless times
my heart blocked out feelings
and yet I would sit
convinced that our friendship was platonic,
convinced that we were safe from it falling apart
when my mind would spontaneously skip the feelings part
and jump straight to us being married
what our home would look like
simple things,
like being in the kitchen with you
doing life,
and making coffee
I could see a married life with you
before my heart ever felt safe enough to date you,
and when my mind had finished playing this fantasy
I would return to the naive belief
that we were *just friends*
I suppress the things I am most afraid of
losing you,
to something as fickle as romance
would be at the top of that list
so yes,
I have pictured a marriage with you
but no,
I do not think I will ever tell you
I jumped out of a plane at 15,000 feet
but risking the loss of you
is far too dangerous for me

the lump in my throat

I just want to cry
while my Father embraces me
because then,
every emotion I've suppressed
the ones that are strong, and the ones that are fleeting
will come to the surface
in the safety of his embrace
only his love,
only his omniscient mind -
his complete understanding of everything I am
and everything I am feeling -
before I have even found a form of expression
can comfort me
for he knows and he sees
the very deepest parts of me
he sees every conflicting thought,
every paradoxical feeling
this treachery makes its way outside of me
escaping only
in the tears that finally fall
as I begin to scream at the sky
only to find
his gentle arms wrapped around me
father, I just want to cry
can you find a way to let me?

i still love you sometimes

I STILL LOVE YOU (SOMETIMES)

I still love
u sometimes

i still love you sometimes.

(sometimes)
i still love u

i still
love you
sometimes...

I STILL LOVE YOU SOMETIMES

sometimes you just need help

how astounding is it
to have made it out of the pit,
because He has lifted you out
to look back on an impossible circumstance,
and to thank God
for the freedom that he has brought you into
because you know that without him,
there is no possible way
that you would ever be standing in this place;
this place of triumphant victory
no,
without him
I would not be standing here
he has brought me out of the place
that was once impossible to escape
and here,
I am abundantly free
from the chains he has broken for me

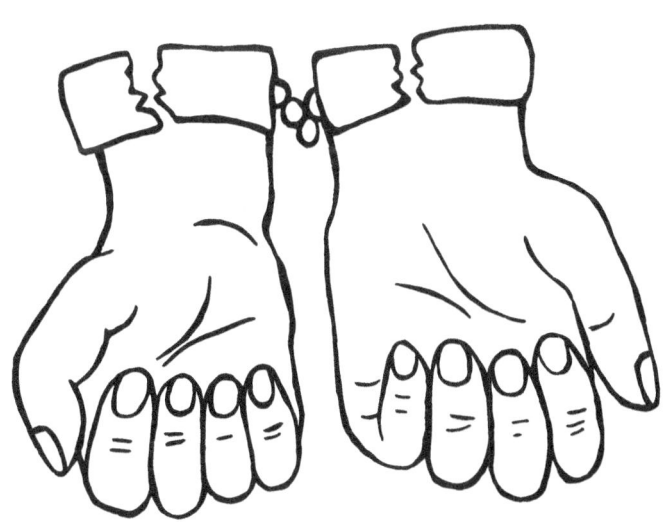

love on my mind

I woke up with love on my mind,
your scent on my skin
the memories of our laughter playing
over and over again
this brought a smile to my eyes
and then the thought occurred to me
that loving you is not good;
that loving you *hurts*
catastrophically
last night was the acception
to countless sleepless nights
spent hurting over you
and now I cannot decide
if you are good for me or if you are the same
because people don't really change
this persona you have been carrying
is not truly you
I know who you are,
and it is not the person I came home to find
you are not the person who broke me,
you lost yourself
and in the pursuit of saving you
I lost myself too
now we are two souls who love each other deeply
but that doesn't mean that I know what to do
and that doesn't mean that what we have is worth saving
I cannot differentiate whether you are the same
or whether you are a poison that runs through my veins
because at times,
loving you hurts
immeasurably
so after all this time,
I find myself waking up with love on my mind, asking:
is the person I tied myself to coming back soon?
is he coming back at all?

stubbornness turned out to be a good thing— who would've thought?

I will be loved with the loyalty
that I so faithfully give
or I will not be loved at all
your version of love,
subscribed to society's standards
is not love at all
in fact,
it is an insult to the word
which all-encompassingly
defines my maker

avoidance is my strong suit

I broke into a million pieces
and I've been pretending like the occurrence which crushed me
never existed
perhaps it is easier this way,
but I've confused my brain
convincing myself that I am not maimed in the slightest
when I am obliterated
how inhuman it is
to experience what I did
and to not grieve properly over the loss of it
I'll explain it like this
the most perfect place in the world to me
is a secluded island covered in golden sunlight
clear blue water
perfect waves
green coverings in the trees
you and me in a cabin just up the beach
this place is in every way and every inch
everything I have desired and hoped for
more even,
more than my wildest dreams
this is happiness made manifest in a place
yet I experienced it in a human
and a hurricane came and took it all away
every perfect inch
every dream that I got to bask within
(for a tragically short time)
was ripped from me

I was smiling ear to ear wide
when all of my dreams lined up,
in you loving me
and then the hurricane came in
and every inch of this place has been washed away
obliterated, like my heart
it's cruel,
that I ever tasted pure and all-encompassing happiness
utterly, completely
totally incandescent
happiness
that was ripped away
when the sun went down one day
and it never came back
walking sunlight came into my life,
and when it left
all there was was darkness
and me
alone in the remains of the hurricane
I cannot hope to pick it all up
my heart is this place,
my heart is the ruins
you were the golden,
you were the hurricane

blocking you was about setting boundaries

maintaining distance from those I love
is not in my nature
I crave intimacy, vulnerability
among all things deep, all things raw
all things blatantly authentic
I do not settle for less than genuine in my relationships
I am finding that the only solution for us right now
is for me to distance myself from you
a solution that seems impossible
and deadly
given my personality,
given what you mean to me
but I need to breathe on my own
I need to be away from your presence
free to be
free to feel
all on my own
the next time I want to text you
I'll write a poem
and then another one
until I can be completely healed
all on my own

hit me

I would rather take a significant beating
than be treated with resentment
the ideal is unjust,
that a person could carry around
a complete and utter lack of forgiveness
for something you've done
and in turn,
do you wrong
because they've gone on hating you
within the confines of their mind
bubbling up in agitation at the smallest of things
when you thought everything was fine
punch me in the face next time
at least then
I can see what you're doing

what do you want?

all he can say is my name,
when apologies are burnt up
when words no longer hold any weight
when excuses count for nothing
all he has left
is to call out my name,
in a pleading way
expressing that he wants me still,
or that he wants *something* still
he doesn't want to leave things this way
but I have nothing left to say
for this betrayal runs so deep,
it has cut to the very core of me
I have no angry words, no screaming rage
I have no emotions to express this time around
no heartfelt expressions of the way he broke me
because this time, he broke my expectations
obliterated my hopes even
and now all that was left
has been disintegrated to ash and dust
I will not give him the chance to wipe my tears this time
I will feel this, and I will break open
but I will do it out of his reach
he cannot reach me anymore
I have no spark left,
no words to say
and when I have lost words
it speaks volumes greater than even words could attain
it requires an almost impossible magnitude
to cause me to walk away
for loyalty and faithfulness define the way I love
but there is nothing left this time,
and all he can say
is my name

I condemn myself for being human

where do you go to get warm
when ice starts to crowd your soul
and the storm comes rolling in
tell me,
where is it that you go?
do you return to the places you have already been
although you know now
that they are crowded with ice
and covered
not with wool blankets
but with ones made of snow

do you go to a friend
do you ever stop to consider
when life makes you cold
that your maker is desperate to hold you?
he is desiring no less
than to have the chance to make you warm again
because the fullness of life is found within him
but will you go to him next time?
will you go to him to get warm
will you ever go to him first
or is he only left in the dust,
subdued to your second pick,
resorted
to your last choice
because he is not here in the flesh
my dear,
he has given you his spirit
so tell me,
when will you give him his rightful seat
in your heart
in your life
and when will I?
his love deserves to be returned with the passion he relentlessly gives
he deserves so much more than this
but for the moments in which I begin to condemn myself
for being insufficient,
for being human
I remember that grace cascades down incessantly
like a waterfall
I am wrapped within his love
and I am enough, because he made me enough
when he died to give me this life, this warmth
this abundance that I get to live within
I will honor him with my love, I will honor him with my life
and today I will start with this;
he deserves that seat in my heart,
the highest one

you should tell them

at least you knew
if I cannot consolidate this loss with anything else
at least there is this one thing;
I know that I will not wake up one day
ridden of the possibility of never telling you again
if the day comes
where I face this world without you in it
at least I can find comfort in this;
you knew,
you knew that I loved you

I did not treat the days like they were never ending
I lived and I loved,
overcoming the fear that is so often crippling
because I know the sting of loss
I know the sting of never getting to say
all of the things I wish I had
because the one to whom I had so much to say
didn't live to see another day
at least I told you,
at least you knew of all the ways I loved you

you're not that special

I want that love
the one that sets off a wildfire
inside of your belly,
kisses you slowly
and tells you
that you are all of the sunlight in the world
I want my heart to stop breaking over you
to meet someone who puts a foggy haze
around our memories
making the time we spent
that is so consuming now
nothing more than insignificant

wrightwood in september

you'll take her up to the mountains
to the place we used to go,
only because you can no longer take me
although this,
she does not know
she won't know
as she sits there in the passenger seat
that though you speak to her
you are only thinking of me
and though you speak of meaning
your words are only empty
you'll intrigue her for a while,
listing off explanations of complexities
letting her into your mind
letting her into what sounds deep
you will only let her see
the facade that you hide behind
so consistently;
a persona of authenticity
you hide behind fabricated joy
while you are catastrophically empty
you'll drive her up to the mountains,
to the place we used to go
and she'll never know
that it is me you wish was sitting
there in the passenger seat
you're filling the spaces I left
with terribly empty things
and I wonder if it is because you are too weak
to repair the damage that you have done to me
she will not fill the space I left within you
no one can,
and you'll realize it soon

when these momentary pleasures
have relented all sense of satisfaction
you'll come after me,
only to find emptiness in the space I used to wait
that has been hollowed out of all meaning
and stripped of every trace of me

do you know what depression feels like?

my emotions are broken
and I have not cried in weeks
which is so incredibly rare for me
I go around seeing the world, feeling the world
empathizing deeply, feeling everything
but I have not cried in weeks

I am drowning in thoughts of insufficiency
I am not qualified
I am not worthy
I am not, I am not
this depressive cycle is relentless in wanting its turn
but all I want
is for it to pass more quickly this time
I thought I had lifted myself out of the pit
but I am sliding back in;
emotionless,
my passion is a dimly lit wick
this is not me
the things I am afflicted with,
they are not me
I am not, I am not these things
no matter how loudly the negativity screams
I recognize these thoughts as lies
I am passionate, I am strong
I am so much more than the sounds that resound
from the pit of despair
my mind has been resting in
I am so much more
than what I am afflicted with
just because you can separate lies from truth
in the light of day
does not mean that it has not been hard
and it does not mean that it has not been dark
you are strong for fighting every day
you are strong for existing despite the resistance
that lives within your brain
you are more than what you are afflicted with
you are strong, you are brave
you are, you are
remind yourself of what you are
even when it is hard,
and even when it is dark

unread poems

I gave my heart to you
open handed
in these poems;
creating acts of devotion
for only your eyes to see,
only to be shelved
and left to become dusty
my devotion should be sought after
and never ignored
you set me down -
and I will not wait for you to want me
when you return to the shelf
that you left me resting on
you will not find me waiting
within this cycle of apathy
people need to be loved intentionally,
not left to collect dust
and neither should my poems be

I would rather walk away than stoop to your level

when someone hurts me
I don't retaliate with my words
I don't search for the right ones to dig deep
in a poor,
and downright sickening attempt,
to hurt them worse than they've hurt me
I don't shock them with the things I say
I simply leave
and hope that my absence
will be enough to leave them wanting

our friend's death shouldn't have been used as a manipulation tactic

I have been tormented
so heavily
that I could not bare to sit under the weight of it anymore
immersed in chaos, and defenseless
I was abused
and when the manipulation could no longer reach me directly
lies began to circle around me
wherever my name was spoken
my character was slandered,
and because my abuser could no longer get to me,
they turned to everyone else in my world
attempting to change the way I was perceived
grasping at straws, they tried to change people's opinion of me
but I know that the Holy Spirit
will vindicate me
He will advocate for me,
because I stand upon truth
your words cannot change that
you stand upon only lies,
which will pass away
how dare you say
that I was cruel to you at our friend's grave
when all I did was comfort you
and pray for you
your words are disturbing and unjust beyond reason
but I stand upon what cannot be shaken
by your tactics and manipulation
all truth is God's truth
and the truth will come out,
without me ever needing
to open my mouth

antisocial personality disorder

I'm starting to think
that hot and cold
is another indication of toxicity
a red flag;
a piercing warning signal
don't call it hot and cold, call it what it is -
it's toxic
to shine like the sun one day
and to be a great thunderstorm the next
this is not healthy,
this is not consistency
neither is it love
you should not whip back and forth like great winds
it is becoming a hurricane around me
"stop it,
stop"
I plead,
"you're killing me"
you go with the winds of human
you go with the winds of impulse
and selfishness
there is no room for reason
in a sea of chaos which runs rampantly throughout your mind
double standards
harsh words
blaming me for the very things that you are doing
apologizing for nothing
tearing me down
word by word

you are so harsh because of the things you have faced
but I am not your doormat to walk over
I am a human meant to be treated with love
and your inability to show grace
is killing me
the sharp edges around you are cutting at me
I am still raw from what you said last week
so please stop it,
or there will be nothing left of me
I stay silent and am wounded continuously
but when I finally get up, the winds only become harsher,
and you cannot hear me
over the noise of the thoughts in your brain
the inability to look past yourself
to love
is what will destroy this in the end

and that is okay

there will be days
when nothing will make sense
you'll be unsure of who you are
nothing stable will surround you
and there will be nothing to help you understand
how you ended up here
there will be days
where you've forgotten your yesterday's
and years even will have dissipated
into an abyss within your brain
all you can remember now are a few vivid moments
you will question everything around you
every belief, every law of the universe,
everything you've ever known
will cease to make sense
yet on these days,
the light is still streaming through
this light will find its way into the darkness
and in the midst of confusion, it will rest upon you
when everything around you seems to be crumbling
there is a steady hand holding your world,
and holding you
all is not lost in confusion and chaos
clear your mind
go to the ocean, go to the mountains
wait on his voice
and the light will come shining through
you will feel its warmth once again
you will feel peace in remembering
that you are not in control
it is not up to you to hold the world
or to understand everything
there will be days where nothing will make sense
and that is okay

remember,
on these days
he has never stopped holding you
even when it got dark, even when it got hard
there was not one day
that he was far

a series of unfortunate events: the glass girl

my innocence was taken from me
not by a man,
but by a friend
when my gentleness was returned
with emotional beatings
when I was resorted to a punching bag
a rug to stomp on
I was turned into someone I could hardly recognize
mangled, maimed, ridden of life
this abuse robbed me of my capacity for intimacy
I had to relearn how to trust
how to resolve conflict
how to feel safe in someone else's love
because your poisonous responses are embedded within me
I expect harshness
I expect abuse
so at the first sight of trouble and lies
my trust is shattered completely
and I freeze, immobilized emotionally
incapable of intimacy
I do not know how to stay and fight
I run
expecting abuse,
I run far from anything that slightly resembles anger and untruth
anything that slightly resembles you
and I crawl into a hole, completely alone
until I realize that maybe not everyone is like you
maybe I was not meant to run
maybe
I can reclaim intimacy
and what was lost can be restored
but in this moment in time,
I am afraid
so I run
I am quick to cut ties,
quick to uncover lies

I am running from potential abuse,
from anything that ever-so-slightly resembles you
my capacity for intimacy was maimed
and my innocence shattered
once upon a time
when I felt safe in someone else's love
and in my vulnerability
was taken advantage of

tell me about what happened in your mind
that night
when I cried tears from deep within my belly
and you tried to hold me
but you weren't really there
tell me about what it feels like
when you want me but don't
when this thing in your mind
that is completely not your fault
tells you that you cannot be and that you cannot feel
I promise,
you are walking sunlight
don't let this darkness cover you
use all of your strength to lift the veil
that tells you this life is not worth living
and in the meantime
I will not walk away
I will do everything in my power to stay

> - *when I was still trying to save you,*
>   *because your excuses were so damn good*

you broke my expectations and then you broke me

it is far worse
to have tasted this happiness
and lost it
than to never have known it at all
you broke every expectation, hope
and dream
surpassing them insurmountably
and then,
you broke me
I still do not understand the wreckage that is within me,
how do I put back together
the wholeness that was once there
before you came and went
quicker than I could take a breath, to take it all in
quicker than I could have ever had a chance to stop you
you were gone
and I am left in the vapor of what will never happen
I wish I never knew of this happiness
you filled me so completely
with things I never asked or hoped for
and now there is a void
you never completed me, you certainly were not my everything,
for a person never could be that for me

but you added good things
extraordinarily
and then left,
quicker than a breath
in one moment you said you would never leave
and the next you were gone
in one moment you said you would fight for me
and the next you gave up
quicker than breathing in
these sentences escaped your lips
I want to marry you,
and then
I cannot be with you
but I cannot process that something could unfold so perfectly
and the next moment all that is left is a vapor in the wind
burnt up in a memory,
a cruel mishappening
my heart has been twirled around and played with like a toy
I am dizzy, disoriented
I cannot get up with these life-altering sentences spinning me around
full of weight, and then heartbreak
I cannot accept a loss
when I do not understand it
and that is why I cannot accept this
I have been spun in circles
both tragically,
and brilliantly

ego isn't everything

I won't stand by,
subject to your pride
as you maim me
because of this repulsive quality
that is puffed up within you
you say no apologies
in regards to what you do
and that
is the most unattractive
insufferable
quality
a person could have
pride
will keep me far from you -
I refuse to be walked over
as your ego is stroked

coming to

one day you'll wake up
and realize that you missed out on my love
it's a wretched thing to say,
but I hope your heart breaks on that day
when you realize that you've lost me,
I hope you feel it deeply
it's a cruel thing to wish for
but you,
ripping my heart out not only once, but repeatedly
deserves to be reconciled with your heart breaking too
you may have been playing games,
but our love was not a game
it was the real thing
and still you left
so I am confident of this;
one day you'll wake up
realizing what you missed
and I hope
that your heart breaks
on that day
because you'll have realized then
that it is too late
I hope the loss of me
cuts to the very core of you
and when you finally see the light
I will be the most profound regret of your life
I hope you feel the way I felt
when you left me alone and I had no one
but you and I both know
(before these wretched words
have even grazed my tongue)
I don't

deep belly laughs

I hold laughter in a high esteem
only because for so long,
I didn't
so I didn't prioritize it, or believe in it really
hardly anything could make me laugh genuinely
but now I've experienced laughter profoundly
and it has forever changed me
deep belly laughs are like perfect rays of sunlight
leaving your jaw aching and your stomach sore
leaving a smile in your eyes
making everything feel okay again
after experiencing it so profoundly,
I cannot go more than a couple of days
without stopping to pray,
asking God for laughter to fill my days
the mornings where I wake and ask for this gift
become the days where he has enriched my life with it
most of all
I ask for a man who will make me laugh
so that my home will be filled with the purity of it
and then
I will not need to seek it out anymore
it will fill the corners of my life richly
there is nothing more beautiful
than the gift of laughter
overflowing zealously,
effortlessly

aha ha
aha ha
haha
haha
HAha
haha
HA

moving back from australia wasn't very much fun

I was alone on that side of the world
I came back to find that I am alone here too
no one was waiting for me
nothing is quite how I left it
relationships, things, structures even
have been shifted dramatically
I don't know how to pick up where I left off
when nothing,
nothing
is in the same place
does anyone love me?
these are the questions I ask myself at 2 am
when self doubt comes creeping in
the most terrifying and treacherous thing
is that someone I love deeply

would just stop
that they could somehow, someday,
just stop loving me
I'm sorry I always ask you if you still love me
something in me believes that love is constantly in jeopardy
maybe if I am perfect I can keep your love,
maybe it was something I had done
that made me lose it before
yet even as I say these things,
I know perfectionism is not the key
for it only ruins things
words of affirmation is the thing my soul craves
because how could it not be?
when the ghosts of past experiences are haunting me
telling me that love could stop at any moment
because it has,
and it does
people walk away sometimes
and often, love is unrequited
I might have to ask again,
when it is next 2 am
do you still love me?
because when you have been abandoned once,
it stays with you
please be patient with me
while I heal from these things
and if I never heal completely,
I pray that you would still love me
remember, if you are like me,
plagued by these things
anyone who is unwilling to love your scars
doesn't deserve your heart
love will heal what the selfish broke within you
and it doesn't have to be a lover who heals you,
it could be a friend

silence is better than bullshit

intentions have become a despicable concept to me,
for they are merely something you plan on doing
yet they are held in such a high regard,
as if they are the most important thing
if he has good intentions but wreaks of passivity
and apathy
he will never pursue you
how despicable, really
that people value intentions so highly
when it is what you actually end up doing
that matters more than the thing you intended on
and never did
good things go unnoticed,
while intentions are sought-after
what is an intention worth
if it stays at that
a promising thought turned dreadful
because it stayed in your head
and never turned into reality
tell her
tell her that what he *does* is the most important thing
not his intentions, not his words even
people walk around this world
wishing to do things and never doing them
they end up in their deathbed
full of empty promises, empty plans
a head full of disregarded intentions

bible reading shouldn't be on your chore chart

communing with your creator
is a life of worship
I used to tick boxes
filling in and filling out all of my responsibilities
until it all shifted
the thought occurred to me that God wants authenticity from me
there is no blueprint for this life; just worship
just love
he wants to commune with us
us with him
this is not religion or legalism
it's living life with my creator
listening to his spirit and his promptings
the knowledge in your head
translates to your heart
then comes out through your life
lived in an honest pursuit of love
reflecting the one who made it all
creator, sustainer God
love him and love people
that was the commission
this has nothing to do with legalism
Jesus is in the business of saving
and you
are in the business of loving

it wasn't worth it

it feels like you're letting our friendship go
even though
you are the only person I have ever believed
when they said they would stay
I knew it -
I knew that feelings always get in the way
they end up changing something that was once pure
into an unmistakably unbearable,
horrible, tragic
loss

liquid courage

I won't be your drunk text
pursue me -
in the daylight and sober
or do not speak to me at all
if you require alcohol to be honest
that is not enough for me
I deserve someone who is unafraid of what they feel;
someone who can love me
authentically

love doesn't exist without grace

to be good to them
even when they are not good to you
to be gentle
even when they are harsh
to pursue
even when they neglect
to nourish their soul
even when they've trampled your own
to be kind
when they have not been
this is love
reading this erupts a rise within my chest
because the sound of it is unjust
to love even when you are being wronged,
it is unjust
but it is love
and love is a choice
you can choose to reflect people's actions as a mirror would
returning to them only what they give
but love is not rooted in fairness
you can choose to love
despite everything
setting yourself aside to see them
and love them
is not easy,
but it is Jesus

it is not enough to want me

you should have lost me the first time
yet I let you come back,
in the name of second chances
I went through the process of healing
and came back to you whole
after you had broken me the first time
after all this time
after all that was between us
was lost and then restored
yet through this horrible process that I've endured,
I've realized that you should have lost me
the first time
when you chose her over me,
it was then that you should have lost me indefinitely
yet here I am, bleeding out,
because it has happened again
and all you can say
is that you want me
but that is not enough,
because I need you to change
and I cannot keep presenting myself whole to you
when all you have done is broken me continuously
not now, not again
a lifetime ago you were healing to me,
but now you are poison to my wounded soul
that can only crawl
as I try to regain my strength
and this time, after all this time,
I am strong enough to walk away
I am drawing a line which says
that you wanting me,
is not enough this time
I need you to love me right
or you don't deserve to be in my life

I will not

we stood by my car
and I smelled alcohol on your breath,
I did not know how much you had
or who you had been with
yet I found myself getting way too close
on purpose
so close, that I could have kissed you again
so close, that I felt your unshaven face graze my mouth
- a feeling I used to hate
yet I craved it this time
because I have missed the feeling
of your skin against mine
I had to back away
and it made my heart break just a little bit
because I want so much more than this
and I will not have you
while you are drunk
and living like this

learning a lesson the hard way
(is hard)

I have learned
that often I do not know what is good for me
and if I was left to myself
to plan out my life
if all of my wishes came true
my life would not be good
and it would not be the way I wanted it to be
the King of Kings knows what I need
far better than me
so now, when the time for wishing comes around,
I'll think of something I want
and then instead of wishing for it, I just pray,
that God would bring all that he has planned for me my way
because often I do not know the first thing about what I truly need
he is infinitely wiser than me
thank God he directs my steps
thank God my wishes did not come true
thank God I get to rest within the truth and the grace
of the life that he has planned for me
each and every day
and not one that I would have created for myself
his plans and his ways
are far better than mine
good thing he is the King of Kings
and not me

being misunderstood hurts like a bitch

to be misunderstood
is heart-wrenching
to be spoken of in whispers and in lies
in darkness, behind closed doors
in unfairness
and untruth
to be seen as something I am not
to be spoken of wrongly
to be accused of the very things
that have been done to me
I ache to be known
I ache to be seen,
in light and in truth
in clarity and in wholeness
in justice
and as me
I ache to be understood
because to be misunderstood
is a form of haunting frustration
that causes pain deep down to my soul
the unjustness of it
reaches my very bones
unravel the gossip, unravel the lies
to truly see people as they are
the cloud will dissipate into thin air
when light and truth are brought near

intimacy doesn't go away all at once

I miss you,
and it is not because I am lonely
and it is not that I have not seen you
when I say *I miss you*, it goes deeper than that
I miss the intimacy that once was
I miss the carelessness of our love
it flowed with ease
you were my watering hole,
never needing to ask for a thing
you rained nourishment down on my soul consistently
and extravagantly
I miss the ease of you and me
I miss it especially,
because now
it feels like it is lost -
lost forever in the wind of what never will be
I want nothing more than our intimacy
you
me
and what we once used to be
because quite frankly,
you are the best thing to ever happen to me

your drifting is more painful than leaving
being here, yet not as close
slowly walking a few steps away from me,
a few steps from where we once used to be
can we reclaim that intimacy?
I swear it,
you are my favorite human to ever exist
I swear
again and again
you are my best friend
I just want to love you
and to be loved by you
the way we used to
so tell me,
is it possible?
or was our friendship just a season,
much like the turning leaves
lost in winter's wind

your coping mechanisms suck

it isn't that I don't want you,
I do
but I am uninterested in things that do not have meaning
and right now, you want to stop thinking,
most days you aren't even feeling
I am not uninterested in you,
the problem is that I want all of you
yet you are unwilling to give me even a fraction,
and I am not the type of person
to settle for something void of meaning, void of feeling
you know this,
you know me
I will not accept surface-level when I crave depth
you say it means something,
but I can feel it has changed
I can feel it when you kiss me
your body close to mine
while your mind is miles away
I need you to find a way to express yourself sincerely
in the meantime, you cannot have me
I will not give in to something that contradicts the values I hold so dearly
I will not abandon myself
nor will I diminish my own value
I am chasing meaning
you are chasing pleasure
and that is not enough for me
I want to be loved radically in the light of day
in godliness, in selflessness
you want to love in the dark
feeding selfishness, gratifying pleasure
and that will never be enough for me
you know this,
you know me
do not treat me
with anything less than authenticity

I deserve an award for this

I know I am starting to love myself
because I did not answer when you called
I did not run back when you beckoned
when I wanted you
I did not move
from this position of protecting my heart
and loving myself first
no matter how hard it has been
I did not waver from my position
of loving myself first
self love is not easy
because you can abuse yourself
and not live to hear any consequences
you can hide a broken heart, easily
but how good is it
to have protected it in the first place
how freeing is it
to be whole again
and to know
that you are in control
of who comes near it

anesthesia

when he told me he didn't believe in love
I waited
and held my breath,
bracing myself for impact
expecting that a wave of catastrophic emotions
would soon hit me
terrified of how this would affect my sleep,
not wanting to deal with the way this would hurt me,
I waited
and the impact never came
I found that some things
are too hard to feel all at once,
and some things are too hard to feel at all
my heart blocked this out to try to save me
for the magnitude was far too great,
it would have been all-encompassing, had I experienced it right then
and right there
when it comes back around,
once it has settled down
I know I will cry from deep within my soul
I will feel this loss in every bone
I will be unable to sleep, unable to find peace
but for now at least,
I am numb

like a dying star

I don't know if it's the distance
or if it's that you're my best friend
maybe some part of me
was always blocking this out of my mind
but I have to tell you about the explosion
that happened inside of me
when you sent me those love songs
that appeared to be declarations
every barrier that I had ever put up,
all of the reinforcements I once held to keep you out
came crumbling down
all of a sudden, every hesitation inside of me combusted
my fear burned up
and I stopped trying to keep you out of the space of my heart
that is so vulnerable that if you held it, you could break it
I fell
but you weren't there to catch me

after death there is new life

what a wonderful day it is
to live
and breathe
and be human;
to be filled with elation
and a heart-warming inspiration
feeling the magic of living all over again
what an extraordinary day it is
to be reminded
that after all that has hindered the light from shining through
you are still here
and you are still you
what a wonderful day it is
to experience something new;
because perhaps today is the day
you'll turn winters corner
to meet spring in its fullness once again
it has been hard
and it has been dark
but it will always get better
there will always be a sunrise waiting on the other side
of the cold dark night
which cast fear deep into your belly
and left you wondering
if it was all worth it,
if anything was worth it
but when you feel the warm sun rays beating onto your skin
when you feel the glory of it sinking in
you'll be reminded of the magic of living
once again
you'll be reminded
after death there is new life
after darkness there is glorious light
after tragic endings there are beautiful beginnings
it isn't over

your story isn't over
you just have to make it through the night
to meet the morning light
and you'll be so glad you made it
when you meet the newness of what is in front of you
and when you begin to fall in love with living
all over again

go

if you want to start building your future,
you're going to have to leave some things behind
and you're going to have to cut some ties
there is power in dreaming,
power in believing
but all of these things come to life
when you first have the strength to go;
when you first take a single step into the unknown
that requires leaving some things behind,
and that requires cutting some ties
you're going to have a bright future,
but you have to go
and going requires leaving
the things that have no room in your future
have no place coming with you
you'll try to pack them in your bags
but you'll realize the weight
of both the old and the new
is too heavy for you
you'll need to let go
you'll need to leave behind what holds you down
disconnecting from it will hurt,
but you'll be making room for the priceless things
and the gold that lies ahead of you
but first,
you must go
you'll find yourself sacrificing the *not-as-good*
for the *better-than-you-can-imagine*
remember,
there is only room for one

lovers OR friends

I have these poems,
but if I have beautiful words
and expressions of heartfelt longings
yet I still do not have you,
then what is it that I am doing?
what have I gained?
is anyone really winning?
I am merely writing about the emptiness inside,
the emptiness that has been resting
ever since you made me fall in love with you
just to watch,
and then decided not to catch me
it's cruel really,
not only can I not have you,
but I got to experience happiness
so brief, and so fleeting
only to be ripped away more quickly than it arrived
it would have been easier
if I never let myself fall
but I always would have wondered
if it was you that my heart was longing for
you do not believe in the very thing that I am drowning without;
yet you made me fall
which unquestionably,
makes you tremendously inadequate
in loving me
I'm drowning in this misery
it requires everything within me
to not get up and run away from you,
away from all of this *feeling*
how can you expect friendship,
after all of this turmoil you have dragged me through?
a lifetime ago
you would be the one to walk me through healing
but not now,
not when it is you who have broken me mercilessly
and perpetually

stay by post malone

I cannot stop picturing
the inside of your room
I walk outside
and half expect you to be waiting there for me
waiting
to apologize
a whiff of nostalgia;
a song on my mind
these incessant reminders take me back
not
to wanting you,
but to facing the reality
in which
ripping you out of me
will not be easy
it will not be like last time
but it will be for the very last time

kissing me was selfish

we had a friendship good and pure
before you kissed me
and then we had something more
a friendship set on fire;
something beautiful, something to be desired
and now
we cannot have a pure friendship,
nor can we have a good relationship
I think us taking that risk
eradicated our capacity for depth
and now what are we left with?
when you look at me
I can't tell if it's love or lust in your eyes
so surface level,
this thing between us has become,
it's killing me
and I do not know if what we have left
is worth anything

if I could give you all my love, I would

I can't let you kiss me
because that would be like saying it is okay,
all of this coming and going
and it is not okay
even though I want to take you in any form I can get
I have to love myself first
and it is unfair to me,
all of this leaving
the inconsistency
is triggering my anxiety
so it really
is not okay
all of your coming and going
you and your depression
and my anxiety all together
in this current state
of them both being inflamed -
no part of this
is good for my sanity
I ask myself
at what point do I stop sacrificing my well-being
for the people I love most?

he better be pretty damn good

I am done with boys and their games
pursue me, when it starts to rain
pursue me when I am in the midst
of a depressive episode
alternating out of anxiety
which then cycles into depression,
as I now experience it
pursue me then -
when it starts to rain
I shine with all of the exuberance of sun rays
but you only get to experience that
if you'll pursue me when it rains
don't let him fool you
carrying a persona of pursuit
don't make it easy,
make him prove that he is willing to do
whatever it takes
to be the one who gets to have you
the one who beholds your heart
if he can endure an uphill battle fought for you
then he just might be good enough for you
don't hide the challenge from him,
let him pursue you when it rains
a *boy*
will fall
a *man*
will rise
carry this with you,
and it will protect your heart
from those too shallow to fight for you

stoner mentality

I know I forgave you
so I am sorry for saying this
but my imagination is running wild
and the things you did with her
when you could have been with me
won't stop playing over again in my mind
I get these wretched, flashing images
clear as daylight
they won't stop causing me this deep pain
I forgive you,
but we will never be the way we could have been
if things had gone differently back then
oh how I wish you would have chosen me
I wish you fought,
but you gave into the flow of things
now the ripple effects of your actions are hitting me,
knocking me down like those reckless ocean waves
the ones that take you under
and spin you so roughly and for so long
that you begin to wonder
if you'll ever be able to come up for air
and I'll need to breathe soon, my dear

I can hardly talk to you about this,
because you will think that because I still feel pain
that I have not forgiven you, which is the farthest thing from true
I just need time for this fragile heart to heal
and I'm discovering that I need someone
who knows how to love me when I am like this;
fragile

my family named me *glass girl*
for a reason
you cannot keep me, you cannot keep anything
if your life's philosophy
is to go with the flow of things
that is not how you obtain anything worth having
and that is not how you keep them,
that is in fact *precisely* how you lose them
in this world you have to fight with a resolve
to be unwavering in the pursuit of what you want
you have to fight for the good things
in life
no flow will teach you how to fight for my heart
if you don't do something soon
you will lose everything,
going with the flow of things

replace me

when I left
you took no time before filling the absence
with other people,
and with exes
I don't know why you didn't decide to fight
all you had to do was apologize
but instead of running after me
you ran into someone else's arms
no matter how toxic
or lonely
they might have been
you filled my absence with empty things
you filled it,
just not with me

and I wish you loved me more than that

all this time I believed you would fight
if it ever came down to this
yet here we are with no goodbyes,
just silence
because you would not put down your pride and fight
I am healing to you,
yet you're injecting the poison that once destroyed you
and I will not wait
for there are some things
you cannot come back from
and I am certain
that by the time you learn this about me
it will be far too late

ignorance is bliss

intuition told me about her
before you did
this hypersensitivity to my surroundings
leaves me painfully tuned in
to what goes over the heads of most
a glance, a phrase
and I am 10 steps ahead
of the lies you have spoken

intuition told me what was going on
when you failed to
this cup is half full
I would rather know
than be 10 months down the road
believing in a love
that has been hollowed out of any trace of meaning

grace

most of the things I do
stem from a place of fear;
fear of being moved
fear of losing you
fear of suffering abuse
I am so terrified
of ever making someone feel a fraction
of what I once endured,
so I destroy myself
in the pursuit of loving perfectly
I do not give myself room to be human
I do not allow myself the grace and compassion
that I relentlessly give to those around me
I am petrified by this cycle of abuse
I do not want to anger anyone
I do not want harshness to come my way
as a result of messing up
so I live every day
scrambling for perfection,
that by it, I might avoid abuse
I am so deathly afraid
of being sucked into that cycle again
of being stuck like I was, under your thumb
I am so afraid
of becoming like you
and treating anyone the way you treated me
all those years ago
you spoke to me
like I was hardly human
you mangled my innocence
and maimed the way I love
the fear you instilled in me
is resting here still
and I do not know if this feeling will ever go away
I am terrified of being me
I am terrified of loving imperfectly
when I fail, like all humans do

I abuse myself
for not being perfect in loving
I always thought it was ironic
that your name depicts the one thing
you are incapable of showing

I hope you are well,

    I hope you are better now

        despite everything

emotionally unavailable

loving you
while you are emotionally unavailable
is turmoil
it felt like hell when you told me
that you spent the love that was meant for me
on all of the wrong people
that you wish you could take it back
and use your unbroken, unused heart
on me
and never on them
it isn't that easy
to just tell me what I mean
because you spent those weighty words on them
and now there is nothing left for me
you know what it's like to say it empty
and you refuse to do that again
you said, in great frustration
that you never meant it with them
that if you told me now,
it would be the truest it has ever been
but you still cannot come around and admit clearly
that you are in love with me
although you have said it
in less words
and in whispers
now
your broken heart is holding you back,
and so is fear
please come back to me when you are whole
I pray this scent will not linger long after you are gone
I need to cleanse my heart and soul
from the pain of you loving me
while being emotionally unavailable
I know I mean everything to you,
yet I cannot have you
I swear this is turmoil,
this is hell

before the clouds came

I've been thinking
it must be
that every time you smile
someone in the world falls in love with it
there is simply no way around seeing something that brilliant
and not falling hard and fast trying to get to it
it almost seems a tease
that that kind of sunshine just goes walking around
completely unaware of the beauty it beholds
and the light
that it carries
you are sunshine aside from all of the cliches
replace the cliches with all of the power of the sun rays
and maybe then you'll understand the power of your beauty,
oh how that smile draws me in

I have spent today
reading through my poems
and editing them
so that they will be ready
for new eyes to see
but as I read old declarations of love,
all I see is naivety
reading over absolutes
that were once prompted by hopefulness

"nothing you ever say
could make me stray away
nothing you ever do
could keep me from loving you"
I realize how wrong I was,
even when I wrote those things,
a part of me knew it could not be true
I knew there was one single line
that would keep me from loving you
and that line was abuse
but I never dared believe you would cross it
there is nobility in the concept of giving your all
for the sake of saving someone who is lost
but in reality,
it is no way to live
for destroying yourself
will never make another person whole
it will only pull you down into the depths of despair
as you rid yourself of life
you will reach out to save them,
to find
all you used to be
dissipated into thin air
you see,
people cannot save people
so I write this part for you:
I leave you in the hands of God
because I cannot save you
and it is not noble to try to
I am uncomfortable reading the declarations I once made
I am declaring one last thing -
they are void
these poems written about you
are ridden of all truth
they carry moments of the past
but that is precisely where I am leaving you

panic attacks are inconvenient

pressure,
it's building
walls,
they're closing
air,
is fleeting
there is not enough air in this space for me to breathe in
deep breaths, deep breaths
I tell myself repeatedly
but the air comes into my lungs to merely skim the surface,
and then returns back to the atmosphere
just as quickly as it entered in
I am left with shallow breaths
which do me no good
in this cycle of relentless anxiety
I have forgotten how to breathe deeply
I have forgotten how to be me
but in this season, I am remembering
however, in this moment,
all I feel is a buzzing
a current so strong
surrounding me,
radiating out of my bones
and a pressure which is unrelenting
a tension which is building
my tear ducts wetten
and I am reminded of what happens
when my anxiety crescendos into this overwhelming,
and yet predictable
pattern
I am reminded of what it is like to reach a point of panic
that is completely outside of the potential to be controlled;
what it is like to be lying on the floor
wondering if anyone in the world is capable of helping
and in that weakness; that loneliness,
simply resorting
to the tear ducts opening

and the water flooding
until it can't anymore
because every ounce has been let out
and you are dried out
ridden of all hydration, and energy, and sanity
because what you just experienced was horrifying
to be lying there on the floor
removed from any measure of control
while your body took over
because of the chaos that was building
because of the pressure that lives within your mind
which led you to the floor
at 2 o clock in the afternoon,
when you had better things to be doing
yes, you'll get up
and yes, you'll recover
but I find myself wondering
if I will ever get to a point
where I can choose to stop the pressure from reaching
this deadly crescendo
which then forces me onto the floor
victim to endless symptoms and merciless thoughts
spiraling, and spiraling, and spiraling
until I have become so dizzy
that I give up
and let it happen
I imagine anxiety as a bully
its foot standing on my belly
pressing me down to the ground,
holding me there
beneath
its
pressure
but I long to be a victor, and not a victim
so I do everything in my power
to cultivate the skill
of harnessing this monster in

the way you lost me

you lost me
not all at once
but in pieces
little by little I withdrew myself
it was as if there was a meter
that used to be full
and you emptied it of my trust,
gradually
so yes, I am here still,
but only in pieces
you can feel it too
the way you still have me
(but don't)
not really

if this is love I don't want it

I love you
is not an eraser for your mistakes -
you must have that confused with
I'm sorry, what can I do to change?
you don't love me more than your pride
you don't love me more than being right
you don't love me enough to comfort me
in the tears you yourself have induced
you don't love me enough to stop inflicting pain
or to at least apologize
for what you have broken within my soul
you don't get to use
I love you
to ease your guilt
when *love* would hold me in this rain,
you are the clouds inducing the storm, the pain
you said,
I love you
I replied,
you don't
because this isn't love
and if it is,
I don't want it

rejection doesn't phase me anymore

whether or not he wants you
is not a question
or a determining variable
in your value
his lack of knowing how to treat you
has more to do with his journey from a boy to a man
than it has to do with you
some never get there
they'll remain lust-oriented and sex-crazed
throughout the duration of their lives
love will frighten the life out of the boy
who never learned how to become a man
he might choose her
and they might look happy
but she is giving him things when the lights go out
that are worth more than your dignity
if he isn't ready for a relationship
if he chooses someone else
even if she's amazing, and even if they are happy,
it does not factor into your value

you have to know,
you are whole on your own
nothing anyone ever says or does could change that
my dear, you have to know this
and I mean *really* know it
deep down to your bones
so when the next boy comes knocking
and then hands you rejection
faster than you could think twice
you already know the answer
when the question floods your mind asking,
am I worthless?
you are worth far more than gold,
you just need to know it
deep down to your bones
and if it is your dignity that he asks for
you will know the answer to that question too
wait for the man who will love you like you are the sun
and do not settle for the one
who just wants to use you

scoundrels

a man who is looking out for your best
will warn you about the nature of men
they will tell you, unashamedly,
that men are dogs
they will tell you not to trust them
I know this is the truth
because one of the only men who can love me purely
is my father,
and this is what he told me
so I formed a philosophy
which I have carried throughout my life;
that men are scoundrels,
until proven otherwise
any man who loves you
will warn you of this too
a day will come
where you'll wish it won't be true
you'll test it with caution, like I did,
and I hope
God, I hope
that the one you choose
proves otherwise
but if he doesn't
remember,
love is a risk that makes falling worth it
your heart will heal
and you will find the strength to try again

dare to be fully known

my hair does not fall the way I want it to
so I tie it up in top knots
hidden, and out of the way
I do this with my personality too
suppressing the parts of me
that don't look quite like I want them to

ew

it's repulsive,
really
the thought of her hands getting to touch you
when all she's done is act as a poison that infects you
it's disgusting,
it's wrong
that something so beautiful
could be resorted to something so impure;
a coping mechanism used to escape depression
done in the hidden hours
with someone you don't even love
you sweet talk her,
into the things she'll do for you
but you hate her
she knows it, everyone knows it
and it's repulsive,
really
using her body for your own pleasure
while she does the same with you
this girl who has caused you nothing but torment
and she *gets* you
again and again
and again
you're addicted to what poisons you
like substances,
you use her
as a form of falsified happiness
like nicotine,
she's no good for you
and I'm starting to believe
you don't love yourself
because you know how to nourish your soul

you know how to get better
but you keep injecting poison into your bloodstream
and it's slowly killing all that was once beautiful within you
it's repulsive,
really
that after all that you once felt for me
you don't give a second thought
to what the knowledge of this will do to me

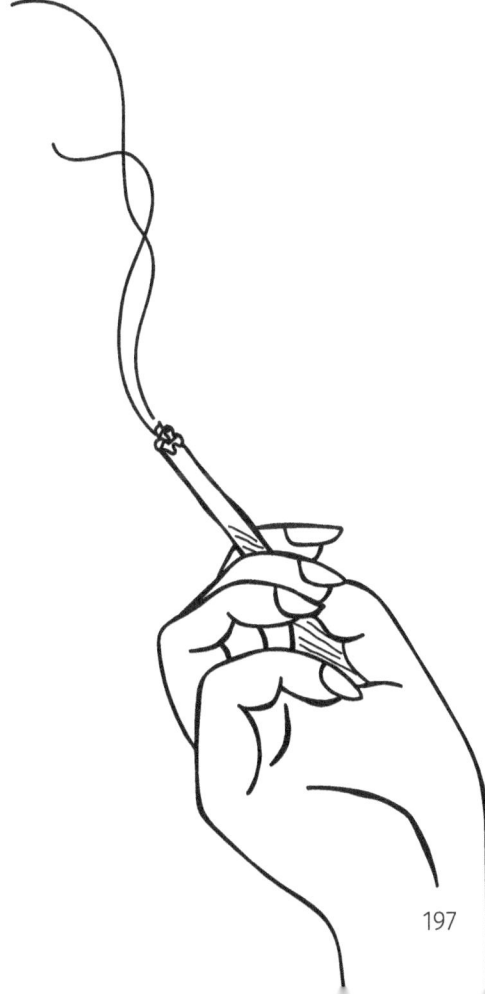

come alive again

you'll feel insufficient on some days,
there will be nights
tears will stream down your face
it will feel impossible to escape the weight,
the sadness,
the thick residue of anxiety resting within you
you'll ache until dawn breaks,
and then you'll face a new day
there will be days like this;
and the nights will feel unending
the season
will feel like a lifetime
you'll wake,
and the sleepless nights will have left their mark on you
bags will be left under your eyes in the daylight
plain enough for all to see the painfulness of this season
but it is okay if they see,
and it is okay
if you feel the weight of darkness
it is okay even
if you cannot lift yourself up from beneath it
because some seasons are like this,
but the leaves will change
and at the end of it you'll be stronger,
you'll be better,
you'll be refined by the struggle
because these seasons stay seasons
the sun will come out again,
and winter's wind will be a memory
when you feel the warmth of the sun on your skin
you'll face the day without bags under your eyes,
and you will be able to say,
"look at what I have overcome
I am here still, and I am okay"
and this is when you will begin
to come alive again

not now not ever

you said
not now, not ever
at least that's what it sounded like
when you said
do not wait for me
because that was the sound
of you not wanting me

looks can be deceiving

when I appear to be the most at peace
is when anxiety is raging within me
I can barely move
I am so still
that I appear peaceful
while I feel anything but peace
I appear serene
because I cannot move in the midst of
anxiety crushing all that is passionate within me
I cannot focus
I cannot think
everything within me is overwhelmed
by the weight of this
I look calm,
but I am drowning
as my movements become slowed
and my voice grows quiet
quiet as a victim who cannot stand up
and rage against the thing that is crushing them
the chaos stills me
resorting me not to peace,
but to paralysis
and silence
yes, I look serene
but I am drowning
my therapist told me I looked at peace
but chaos was raging violently within me
and as soon as I opened my mouth
I broke open
breaking the persona
of peace
and calling anxiety into the light
where someone stronger than me
would fight it

the one thing

my mind works obsessively
within these parameters set by anxiety
everything in my life has to be in the perfect order
but I breathe deep in these poems,
because they are *the one thing*
that doesn't have to

endless love

I've been wondering lately
if endless love
is merely a concept created by fiction novelists
and poets more creative than me
an idea so abstract -

that a person could fill the holes within you;
that another human being could start repairing
all of the damage that has been done to you
although it is true,
that God uses people to show the love
which he himself embodies
although image bearers are God-reflecting,
love-reflecting
those holes
can only be filled by God himself
loving perfectly
never will be
not from a human's heart
not on this side of eternity
loving endlessly?
that is not up to you or me,
that remains in the hands of the one you love
and they can choose to leave
to stop
to not love you anymore
so I wonder
if endless love could ever be anything but a gamble
that ends up lost
because it requires faithfulness and trust
that so many abandon for the sake of anything but love
I've experienced holding my heart between open hands,
to give to a man
who forsook it
and where he was meant to be healing to me
he only left more scars
love leaves a lasting mark,
every time you risk for it
with an open heart

how dare you

my heart is not versatile
it does not come and go,
changing with ease like the seasons do
it needs time and space to heal
and
it needs time away from you,
too
I cannot hear
I'm falling in love with you
and a week later,
the same voice that was once safe
and warm
is now muttering
I cannot be with you
in one sentence
your voice tore down trust
that took years to build
I watched your lips move
but no sound reached my ears -
I could only hear my heart reaching impenetrable volumes,
screaming
that I was not safe with you here,
I was not safe after all
I will not go with your rigid rhythm,
I am making my own
I will flow in and out of life unattached from you
how dare you treat me like a cat
you,
dangling a string over me
back and forth,
back and forth you swayed
and it almost killed me
it's too bad for you,
I am no longer mesmerized by your rhythm

no one can do what you can do

you might never be brave the way that she is
or pretty like her
or strong like her
in fact,
you will *never* embody those things
the way that she does,
because you have a uniqueness about you;
you will be brave, and pretty, and strong
never the way that she is,
but the way that you are
and the way that you have always been
you don't want to live in the fabric that was created for her
when you can extravagantly be you;
for no one can do what you can do
no one can embody bravery
no one can embody beauty
and no one can embody strength
quite like you

I'm starting to think nicholas sparks is a liar

what good is all of this lovesickness?
romance is far too inconvenient
it is weighing on me,
occupying space in my heart and mind
that could be filled with happier things
I'm bleeding and there is no one here to save me
you used to be a safe haven
yet now it is you who is causing my wound
so tell me,
what good is romance?
look at what it is doing
I do not want to feel like this
I cannot fall asleep at night because I am terrified of being alone
with a wounded heart
what good has romance ever done me?
lovesickness just keeps me
from happier things
I want to spend my days focused on what I have
not on what I do not
I want my head to hit the pillow
and to smile, for all of the good that is in my life
instead, my head hits the pillow
and my thoughts race
and my heart aches
and I wonder again and again
if I could ever have you
if I could ever be happy
if someone could ever love me,
or if I am unlovable
I do not want to feel this way
tell me,
what good is it?
what good is love?

get up

I don't want anxiety
to have a rule over my life anymore
it seems as though every comforting
and rational voice
turns to a whisper
while this thing screams into my ears,
and makes its way
into every corner of my body
it blocks out every other sound
I know by now
there is nothing it will not touch
body, mind, spirit, emotion
it will consume everything if I let it
still I resolve to say
I will fight every day,
and in the end
I will not be consumed by this

irreconcilable contradictions

he was my safe place
until he wasn't safe
in familiarness, in routine
I would duck to find refuge within him
until one day I came and found that the safety was gone
and the warmth was fleeting
the one who once shielded my pain
began inflicting it
how paralyzing it is
to enter into the place you go to get warm
and instead are visited with a snowstorm
shock kept me there,
in the doorway
gaping
but now I have gathered myself enough to see
that although I once ran to him,
the time has come to run from him
he is not my safety
this place I have entered
is the farthest thing from safe
when my heart is hanging on by a thread,
when I am trembling violently from within
I cannot go on convincing myself
that the damage has not been done
when I am living like this:
broken,
though I came to him whole
I cannot keep saving him
I need to save myself this time,
I need to save myself again
because I am not sure
how many times I can break
and put myself together again

(not) worth the wait

you didn't listen to me
when I said I had to leave
you didn't understand how it got to this point
which is outrageous to me
let me lay it out for you clearly;
you have broken my heart continuously
I have too much self respect
to sit and watch this unfold again
you say one thing and do another
tell me,
why is it that you say you want to be with me
then date someone else
you say you're falling in love with me
while you're passed out in someone else's bed
you say you don't want to lose me
then barely speak to me
my ears are deaf to these excuses,
I have waited patiently for you to change
and once this door closes,
it will not open again

please let me get what I want this time

the next time I fall in love
I hope to God that it's for real
I hope it's the kind of love
that flows both ways
with the great force of ocean waves
not a still tap that simply goes drip drip
I hope that the next time I fall in love,
it will be for the last time
because I will have met
the one my soul has been aching to find
the stars will shine brighter,
the sun will set all the more brilliantly
when you live life with the love of your life
right by your side
God, don't let my heart break again
don't let it ache
while I cry myself to sleep at night,
I'm vowing right now to guard this heart of mine
and to only give the key
to the one who will never leave
I hope,
oh God,
that the next time I fall in love
it will have been for the last time,
please let it be the last time

you're the way you are for a reason

what a shame it would be
to miss out on yourself entirely
and to never truly know
who you were created to be
what a shame it would be
to spend your life resembling their reflection,
and replicating their personality
you were made to be beautiful
you were made to be unique
you are *exactly right*
and *precisely*
who you are meant to be
don't rip out your roots,
nourish them
don't conceal yourself, never to be seen
bloom, in the light of day
bloom for everyone to see
all that you are
and all that you were made to be
if you replant yourself in their soil,
you won't grow correctly
but here,
in the soil of your soul
you'll grow marvelously

~~PERFECT~~

~~DOESN'T~~

~~EXIST~~

you don't need
a perfect body
to be beautiful
you don't need
to be less of who you are
and more like them
to be delighted in
we tell ourselves these lies;
that if I looked like her -
if I was less intense
and had more curves
that he would have stayed
you tell yourself
that your love wasn't enough to keep him
that you were simultaneously not enough
and too much
to keep him intrigued
longer than a moment
long enough to last a lifetime
but the truth is
if a shoe does not fit
that does not mean that something was wrong with it
you do not need to be different
you do not need to be less
or more
to be loved
because you don't have to be perfect to be loved;
after all,
perfect doesn't exist

you don't know me

when you speak about me,
do not speak as if you know who I am
when you only knew who I was
a lifetime ago
don't you dare contain
all the ways I've grown
for the person I am now
couldn't bare to rest
within the shadow of who I used to be;
no,
you hardly know me
for you only knew
of my beginnings.

acknowledgements

Thank you to the first people I ever felt safe enough to share my poetry with. You filled me with the confidence and the courage to be braver than I had ever been before. This book would not be here today without the words of encouragement and the belief that was instilled in me in those painfully vulnerable moments.

Krista Esse, thank you for leading by example and showing me that anything is possible. You are my heart and soul, and you always will be. Thank you for your beautiful art that this book would not be the same without.

Courtney Brubaker, thank you for being a lifeline for me in the season that most of these poems were written. You are and always will be my family.

Katie Conover, thank you for reading each and every one of my poems, building my website, and empowering me in a way that no one ever has before. You have been there in every detail of this project and I am honored that your creative thumbprint is on this.

Sam Sadowsky, thank you for your selfless intentionality and the hours you spent working with me on this project.

To my family, thank you for teaching me valuable life lessons and playing an instrumental role in molding me into the person I am today.

Most of all, I want to thank God for giving me the words, the ability to write, and the experiences that these poems were birthed out of. I truly believe that each and every one of these poems was placed in my mind and meant to be written down for a specific person to read. I am abundantly thankful for that.

about the author

Jaclyn Esse is a self-taught poet and creator of a streetwear brand called Perfect Doesn't Exist based in Southern California. She currently works as an independent contractor for a network marketing company and leads a team of people.

Jaclyn's poems are focused on topics such as mental health, self love, growth, and pursuing authentic relationships with God and other people. Through themes of empowerment, she expresses how her life experiences have molded her into the person she is today. She uses poetry to make connections through shared experiences, trauma, and emotion-- putting words to what most feel but cannot express.

Combining her love of poetry and fashion, she turned Perfect Doesn't Exist into an online streetwear brand that carries hoodies, crewnecks, shirts, tote bags, beanies and phone cases. Perfect Doesn't Exist is a way for the message behind her poetry to be spread, encouraging anyone who sees it to have grace for themselves and their art.

@ jaclynnoelle7 | @perfectdoesntexistco

www.ingramcontent.com/pod-product-compliance
Lightning Source LLC
Chambersburg PA
CBHW021946290426
44108CB00012B/977